STECK-VAUGHN GED
Literature & the Arts

EXERCISE BOOK

VIRGINIA A. LOWE

STECK-VAUGHN COMPANY
ELEMENTARY • SECONDARY • ADULT • LIBRARY

About the Author

Virginia A. Lowe is an author, teacher, editor, and test-writer in the field of adult education. Virginia holds an M.A. in English from the University of Oregon and is pursuing doctoral work in folklore at Indiana University. Virginia has written test items for the GED Testing Service and has written and edited GED preparation books. She has also been an ABE/GED instructor in Indiana. Virginia has published articles on historical aspects of folklore.

Staff Credits

Executive Editor:	Ellen Northcutt
Supervising Editor:	Tim Collins
Senior Editor:	Julie A. Higgins
Design Manager:	John J. Harrison
Cover Design:	Rhonda Childress
Electronic Production:	Jill Klinger

ISBN 0-8114-7368-6

Copyright © 1996 Steck-Vaughn Company

All rights reserved. No part of the material protected by this copyright may be reproduced or utilized in any form or by any means, electronic or mechanical, including photocopying, recording, or by any information storage and retrieval system, without permission in writing from the copyright owner. Requests for permission to make copies of any part of the work should be mailed to: Copyright Permissions, Steck-Vaughn Company, P.O. Box 26015, Austin, Texas 78755.
Printed in the United States of America

4 5 6 7 8 9 DBH 99 98

Contents

To the Learner 2

Unit 1: Popular Literature 4
    Fiction 4
    Nonfiction 12
    Poetry 18
    Drama 27

Unit 2: Classical Literature 32
    Fiction 32
    Nonfiction 36
    Poetry 39
    Drama 45

Unit 3: Commentary 48
    Literature 48
    TV and Film 52
    Visual Arts 56
    Performing Arts 59

Simulated GED Test A 62
    Analysis of Performance Test A 73

Simulated GED Test B 74
    Analysis of Performance Test B 86

Answers and Explanations 87

Suggestions for
Additional Readings 106

Acknowledgments 107

Answer Sheet 109

To the Learner

The *Steck-Vaughn GED Literature and the Arts Exercise Book* provides you with review and practice in answering the types of questions found on the actual GED Interpreting Literature and the Arts test. It can be used with *Steck-Vaughn GED Literature and the Arts, Steck-Vaughn Complete GED Preparation*, or other appropriate materials. Cross references to other Steck-Vaughn books are supplied for your convenience on exercise pages. This book has two sections: practice exercises and simulated tests.

Practice Exercises

The practice exercises are divided into three units: popular literature, classical literature, and commentary on the arts. The popular literature section contains practice in fiction, nonfiction, poetry, and drama. These excerpts are taken from contemporary literature. The classical literature section also contains practice in fiction, nonfiction, poetry, and drama. These selections are written by well-known authors who have earned a permanent place in literary history. The final section, commentary on the arts, contains reviews of books, TV and films, art, and musical performances. These reviews contain both facts and opinions that require careful attention.

Simulated Tests

This exercise book contains two complete full-length Simulated GED Literature and the Arts Practice Tests. Each Simulated Test has the same number of items as the actual GED Test and provides practice with similar item types as found on the GED Test. The Simulated Tests can help you decide if you are ready to take the GED Literature and the Arts Test.

To get the most benefit from the Simulated Test Section, take each test under the same time restrictions as for the actual GED Test. For each test, complete the 45 items within 65 minutes. Space the two examinations apart by at least a week.

Reading Passages The reading passages are always introduced with a question that may help to guide your thinking about the passage. Half (50%) of the passages are popular literature, 25% are classical literature, and 25% are commentary on the arts. When you are reading a drama passage, be sure to read the stage directions carefully. Poems are usually relatively short, but take time to think about and understand the poem. Rereading the poem entirely may be helpful.

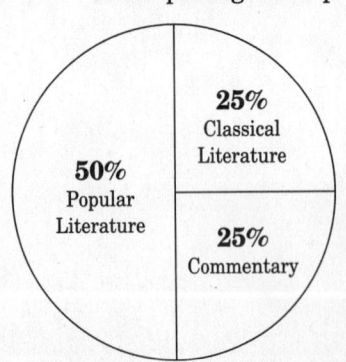

The GED Interpreting Literature and the Arts Test examines your ability to understand, apply, analyze, and evaluate information in four literature areas and commentary.

All of the questions on the GED Interpreting Literature and the Arts Test are multiple choice. You will not be tested on your knowledge of literature, but rather on your ability to understand, interpret, and analyze what you read. Following is an explanation of the four types of questions that you will practice in this book, and that are found on the GED Literature and the Arts Test.

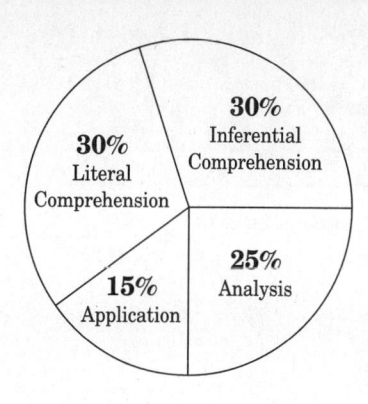

1. Literal Comprehension: These items require you to restate information and summarize ideas.

2. Inferential Comprehension: These items ask you to draw conclusions and infer. They also require you to identify implications of what you read or determine cause and effect of events, feelings, or ideas.

3. Application: These items require you to apply information or ideas to a situation that differs from the one in the passage. Questions may be similar to, "How would the author feel about...?" You must use the information provided to problem-solve.

4. Analysis: These items require you to examine the elements of style and structure in an excerpt and to determine how these elements relate to the excerpt's final effect.

Analysis of Performance Charts

After each Simulated Test, an Analysis of Performance Chart will help you determine if you are ready to take the GED Interpreting Literature and the Arts Test. The charts give a breakdown by content area (popular literature, classical literature, and commentary on the arts) and by question type (literal comprehension, inferential comprehension, application, and analysis). By completing these charts, you can determine your own strengths and weaknesses as they relate to the literature and the arts area.

Answers and Explanations

The Answers and Explanations section gives complete explanations of why an answer is correct, and why the other answer choices are incorrect. Sometimes by studying the reason an answer is incorrect, you can learn to avoid a similar error in the future. A list of recommended readings is included following the Answers and Explanations. You can use the books and periodicals listed in this section to gain additional experience reading selections similar to those on the GED test.

Correlation Chart

The following chart shows how the sections of this exercise book relate to sections of other Steck-Vaughn GED preparation books. You can refer to these other two books for further instruction or review.

CONTENT AREAS	Popular Literature	Classical Literature	Commentary on the Arts
BOOK TITLES Steck-Vaughn GED Literature and the Arts	Unit 1	Unit 2	Unit 3
Steck-Vaughn GED Literature and the Arts Exercise Book	Unit 1	Unit 2	Unit 3
Steck-Vaughn Complete GED Preparation	Unit 6, Popular Literature	Unit 6, Classical Literature	Unit 6, Commentary

Unit 1 Popular Literature

Fiction

Directions: Choose the best answer to each item.

Items 1–3 refer to the following excerpt from a short story.

HOW DOES BERT REALLY FEEL?

When he found out that Manny was going to die, Bert didn't feel the way he knew he should, the way he knew everyone else would feel. Friends for
(5) twenty years, yet the sense of impending loss was tempered…by what? Bert was sorry for Manny, but thankful that it was Manny and not him. Where was the grief?

What Bert did feel was a sense of
(10) exhilaration, and he couldn't understand it. He tried to feel differently but could barely control his excitement; he was actually looking forward to telling everyone the news. He was already
(15) planning Manny's funeral. …

Bert pictured the funeral. And a grand event it would be. He could see the twenty-four white cabs all freshly washed and shined, moving in a dignified
(20) procession behind the contrasting black funeral cars. People would stop what they were doing and look.

"They must have really respected that guy," they'd say. "He must have been a
(25) good cab driver."

Bert got choked up just thinking about it. There would be black crepe on all the aerials. He'd talk to Conklin about it. Hell, the guys would go for that, somebody had
(30) probably suggested it already. They could sell it to Conklin because it would be good advertising, Bert reasoned. But when Bert suggested it Conklin practically bust a gut.

"Do you realize how much it would cost
(35) us to do that? We'd have to pass almost a thousand calls to the opposition if we took all our cars off the road for an afternoon, and you can bet there would be a certain percentage of that business we'd never get
(40) back. Besides, Mankiewitz isn't dead yet."

"He will be."

"I don't know. I had an uncle they gave up on a couple of times. He's still living."

"Have you seen him lately?" Bert knew
(45) the answer but he hoped he might embarrass Conklin a little. That afternoon Manny's eyes had been kind of dull and lifeless, and his two-day beard was like a skiff of snow on his face.

W. P. Kinsella, "Mankiewitz Won't Be Bowling Tuesday Nights Anymore," *Shoeless Joe Jackson Comes to Iowa*.

1. Which of the following best describes Bert's relationship with Manny?
   (1) Bert is the funeral director for Manny's funeral.
   (2) Bert is Manny's boss.
   (3) Manny is Bert's boss.
   (4) Bert and Manny are longtime friends.
   (5) Bert is Manny's only living relative.

2. According to the excerpt, Bert was most concerned about Manny's
   (1) absence from work
   (2) death
   (3) funeral
   (4) layoff
   (5) visit from Conklin

3. Which new profession would best fit Bert's personality?
   (1) clergyman
   (2) physician
   (3) sympathy card writer
   (4) special events director
   (5) ad writer

Items 4–7 refer to the following excerpt from a novel.

WHERE ARE THESE PEOPLE GOING?

Taylor is getting a long, hard look at someone's bald spot. He has reclined his seat to a point where he's closer than a dinner plate, maybe twelve inches from her face. The top of his head is covered with fine, almost invisible fur that lies flattened in a complicated pattern, like a little prairie swept by a tornado. It reminds Taylor of a theory Jax once told her about, that (10) humans evolved from some sort of water ape and spent the dawn of civilization in a swamp. Streamlined hair patterns are supposed to be the proof, but Taylor wonders as she stares, Does that mean (15) we moved through the water headfirst? Could be. Kids move through the world that way, running into things with the tops of their heads. This man has a scar up there, no doubt forgotten through the decades (20) until now that it's lost its cover.

The pilot comes on the intercom again. He's a chatty one; right after takeoff he introduced himself as "your captain," and Turtle's eyes grew wide. She asked Taylor (25) if he only had one hand. Now, after mulling it over the whole afternoon, it dawns on Taylor that the only captain Turtle knows about so far is Captain Hook. She may never get on a plane again without (30) envisioning a pirate at the helm.

Captain Hook now explains they are passing over the Mississippi River, and that if he can do anything to make the passengers more comfortable they should (35) just let him know. Frankly, although she doubts the captain can help her out here, Taylor doesn't feel comfortable being intimate with a stranger's hair loss. She doesn't even know the top of Jax's head (40) this well. She's looked at it, but not for three and a half hours.

Turtle is finally sleeping. She seems to be coming down with a cold, and really needed a nap, but was so excited she sat (45) for hours with her face pressed hard against the window. When the window turned icy cold, even when there was nothing to see but a vast, frosted field of clouds spread over a continent, rutted (50) evenly as if it had been plowed, Turtle still stared. Everybody else on the plane is behaving as though they are simply sitting in chairs a little too close together, but Turtle is a child in a winged tin box seven (55) miles above Planet Earth.

Taylor hasn't flown before either, and for the first few hours she felt the same excitement. Especially when they were taking off, and before, buckling up, (60) watching the stewardess show how to put on a yellow oxygen mask without messing up your hair. And before that, leaving the airport: walking behind Turtle down the sloping hallway to the door of the plane, (65) stepping across from solid ground to something unknown, furtively checking the rivets around the door, but what can you do? She has no choice but to follow her daughter into this new life she's (70) claimed from a fortune cookie.

Barbara Kingsolver, *Pigs in Heaven*.

4. According to the excerpt, for much of the trip Turtle is
   (1) scared of flying
   (2) too excited to sleep
   (3) interested in a man's bald spot
   (4) afraid of the captain
   (5) too nervous to talk to her mother

5. Captain Hook is
   (1) the pilot's name
   (2) the rest of Jax's name
   (3) the man in the next seat
   (4) Turtle's father
   (5) a character in a pirate story

6. Which of the following best describes the other people on the plane?
   (1) They stare at Turtle.
   (2) They don't understand the captain's announcement.
   (3) They have probably flown before.
   (4) They are all sleeping.
   (5) They seem excited to be flying.

7. Based on the information in the excerpt, Taylor and Turtle are most likely going
   (1) to live in a new place
   (2) to visit grandparents
   (3) on vacation
   (4) to visit Jax
   (5) home

Items 8–11 refer to the following excerpt from a novel.

IS THE TRAIN COMING?

The three of us just sat looking across the water then. And then we heard the next northbound freight coming, and he stood up and got ready; and he said we could
(5) watch him but we better not try to follow him this time, and we promised, and we also promised to go to school the next morning.

So then we came back up the embankment, because the train was that
(10) close, and he stood looking at us, with the guitar slung across his back. Then he put his hands on our shoulders and looked straight into our eyes, and you knew you had to look straight back into his, and we
(15) also knew that we were no longer supposed to be ashamed in front of him because of what we had done. He was not going to tell. And we were not going to let him down.

Make old Luze proud of you, he said
(20) then, and he was almost pleading. *Make old Luze glad to take his hat off to you some of these days. You going further than old Luze ever dreamed of. Old Luze ain't been nowhere. Old Luze don't know*
(25) *from nothing.*

And then the train was there and we watched him snag it and then he was waving goodbye.

Albert Murray, *Train Whistle Guitar.*

8. To whom does the repeated <u>he</u> in this passage refer?

   (1) the narrator
   (2) the narrator's father
   (3) part of the <u>we</u> in the last sentence (line 26)
   (4) the engineer of the train
   (5) old Luze

9. Two of "the three of us" (line 1) are probably

   (1) hoboes
   (2) criminals
   (3) running away
   (4) schoolchildren
   (5) ashamed of their friend

10. What is the best reason that many of the sentences in the first two paragraphs are very long?

    (1) to emphasize the suspense of waiting
    (2) because there is no dialogue
    (3) as a contrast to the first sentence
    (4) to contrast with the sentences of dialogue
    (5) because the ideas expressed are complex

11. What action is described by "snag it" (line 27)?

    (1) waving from the train
    (2) getting on the train
    (3) going up the embankment
    (4) waiting for the train
    (5) watching the train from the embankment

Items 12–13 refer to the following excerpt from a novel.

WHY IS THE MEMORY SO PAINFUL?

    I'd done a lot of thinking about Lee in the last year, remembering him the way he was at four and five and six. Partly, I imagine, because the news of his mom got
(5) me thinking about the old days, but some because he was the only little kid I've ever been around and there'd be lots of times when I'd think, That's what our kid'd been like now. That's what our kid'd be saying
(10) now. And in some ways he was good to compare to, in some ways not. He always had a lot of savvy but never much sense; by the time he started school he knew his multiplication tables all the way to the
(15) sevens, but never was able to figure why three touchdowns comes to twenty-one points if a team kicked all their conversions, though I took him to ball games till the world looked level. I remember—let's see,
(20) I guess when he was nine or ten or so—I tried to teach him to throw jump passes. I'd run out and he'd pass. He wasn't none too bad an arm, either, and I figured he should make somebody a good little
(25) quarterback someday if he would get his butt in gear to match his brains; but after ten or fifteen minutes he'd get disgusted and say, "It's a stupid game anyway; I don't care if I ever learn to pass."

Ken Kesey, *Sometimes a Great Notion*.

12. Why does the narrator think Lee didn't have "much sense" (line 12)?

   (1) because Lee couldn't learn multiplication
   (2) because Lee wasn't interested in football
   (3) because Lee was too little to have sense
   (4) because the boy would never become a good quarterback
   (5) because the boy had a lot of savvy

13. Which of the following is not a reason for the narrator to think about Lee?

   (1) The narrator had known Lee's mother.
   (2) Lee had been one of the few children the narrator had known.
   (3) The child the narrator never had might have been something like Lee.
   (4) Lee reminded the narrator of his youth.
   (5) The narrator had spent a lot of time with the boy.

Items 14–15 refer to the following excerpt from a short story.

WHAT MAKES THIS BOY STUDY?

    When school began in September, before Cohen would once again suggest giving the bird the boot, Edie prevailed on him to wait a little while until Maurie adjusted.
(5) "To deprive him right now might hurt his school work, and you know what trouble we had last year."
    "So okay, but sooner or later the bird goes. That I promise you."
(10) Schwartz, though nobody had asked him, took on full responsibility for Maurie's performance in school. In return for favors granted, when he was let in for an hour or two at night, he spent most of his time
(15) overseeing the boy's lessons. He sat on top of the dresser near Maurie's desk as he laboriously wrote out his homework. Maurie was a restless type and Schwartz gently kept him to his studies. He also
(20) listened to him practice his screechy violin, taking a few minutes off now and then to rest his ears in the bathroom. And they afterwards played dominoes. The boy was an indifferent checker player and it was
(25) impossible to teach him chess. When he was sick, Schwartz read him comic books though he personally disliked them. But Maurie's work improved in school and even his violin teacher admitted his
(30) playing was better. Edie gave Schwartz credit for these improvements though the bird pooh-poohed them.

Bernard Malamud, "The Jewbird."

14. How could Schwartz be best described?

   (1) a well-trained pet
   (2) an unwelcome visitor
   (3) an intellectual talking bird
   (4) an indifferent tutor
   (5) an avid chess fan

15. The author probably intends the reader to see this scene as

   (1) realistic
   (2) melodramatic
   (3) slightly fanciful
   (4) slightly mysterious
   (5) totally unbelievable

Items 16–19 refer to the following excerpt from a novel.

WHAT'S ALL THE FUSS ABOUT?

One A.M. Peter and July broke into the captain's cabin. The curtain was pulled across the berth, a heavy blue cambric which also covered the porthole, shutting
(5) out the sun when the captain wanted to sleep. Tentatively Peter pulled back the curtain, possessed by the wild notion that Captain Regan was hiding in his bunk and would leap up and choke him. The berth
(10) was empty, of course. In the hanging locker he found what they were looking for—the wide-brimmed black hat, a pistol and a smooth-bore gun. Peter threw the musket to July and shoved the pistol into
(15) his waistband. Then he picked up the hat, his hands shaking. Suppose it didn't fit? Suppose it was too big and fell down over his eyes blinding him?

"What's so funny?" July asked, a frown
(20) on his handsome face at the absurdity of anything being funny on this menacing day.

"The captain's hat. She's a perfect fit."

"Naturally. You both fatheads."

Peter grinned. "Let's get on back—"
(25) Brother Man interrupted him, sticking his big head through the door. "You better hurry up on deck, Peter. Turno's about to kill Aaron."

With an oath Peter hurried topside. The
(30) burly fireman had cross-eyed Aaron backed up against the rail, choking him. The crew was hollering, "Let him go," but making no move to interfere except for Stretch.

"For God's sake, man," Stretch yelled,
(35) grabbing Turno's arm.

The fireman snatched it free and socked him. The blow dropped Stretch to his knees. Turno lifted Aaron off his feet while squeezing his neck, the deckhand's eyes
(40) rolling around like loose pebbles in his head. "Loose him," Peter yelled running forward. He snatched the pistol from his waistband and reaching the fireman jabbed it into his side. "I ain't fooling,
(45) Turno. Let him go."

Turno released Aaron so suddenly that the man stumbled and fell. Kneeling on the ground and rubbing his neck he blubbered, "He were gon kill me, Peter."

(50) The fireman stared at him with contempt. "You is a lie. I was gonna toss you overboard only half dead and let the sharks finish you off."

Louise Meriwether, *Fragments of the Ark.*

16. Which of the following best describes the situation in the excerpt?

   (1) a fishing trip
   (2) a practical joke
   (3) a shipwreck
   (4) a trip on a ferry
   (5) a mutiny

17. When Peter and July broke into the captain's cabin, they found

   (1) a blue shirt
   (2) two guns
   (3) the captain
   (4) two hats
   (5) a fireman

18. It can be inferred from the excerpt that the leader of this group is

   (1) Peter
   (2) July
   (3) Aaron
   (4) Stretch
   (5) Captain Regan

19. Turno's words and actions suggest that he is a

   (1) weakling
   (2) prankster
   (3) bully
   (4) leader
   (5) negotiator

Items 20–22 refer to the following excerpt from a novel.

WHAT DOES JOE KNOW?

Joe was a short, dark-haired Iranian who passed himself off as Hispanic. He spoke fluent Spanish and had kept the previous owner's name, Jose Lopez, on
(5) the door. Marti was certain that despite

Joe's caution, nobody in the neighborhood cared about his heritage.

Joe nodded and smiled a lot. "Yes ma'am. Certainly. I will look at the pictures (10) again. The other officers, the ones in uniform, they show me the pictures, too."

She stood on the customers' side of the counter. Candy had to be a big seller. There was an incredible variety, much of it (15) costing a nickel. She hadn't seen anything like it since she was a kid. She could almost taste the jawbreakers and Mary Janes.

Joe looked at the photographs of R. D., both dead girls, and a few anonymous (20) perps currently doing time in Joliet. She had added morgue shots of Danny Jones and Ruth Price and a mug shot of Glodine, one of the women associated with R. D. who had been arrested once for prostitution.

(25) Joe identified Teresa and Carmen. He hesitated when he came to the snapshot of Price. "This is the woman who was killed last night?"

"Yes."

(30) He seemed to want to tell her something. She waited.

"I have seen her."

"Was she a customer?"

Again he hesitated.

(35) "She's dead," Marti reminded him. "What can you tell me?"

"This old woman, she comes through the alley. On Thursday. Other old ones come too."

(40) He seemed uneasy and moved to the rear of the store. He stopped at a long case filled with fruit and vegetables. Everything looked fresh except for some produce stacked on an unrefrigerated shelf.

(45) "On Thursday, what was delivered on Monday I sell at half price." He pointed to the unrefrigerated produce, a little wilted but not spoiled. "What is left when I am ready to close I put out with the garbage. (50) In a box, separate. The old ones come. They take it."

"I could still sell," he said, "but I put out. In my country, there is hunger. Here there are so many rules. Is wrong, illegal that I (55) put it out? I do not put it with the rest of the garbage, I keep it separate. The old ones know."

"It's okay," she assured him, unwilling to get involved with health-code violations. (60) "You can put out whatever you want and package it any way you want to." At least she thought so. "There are soup kitchens, churches, and other places that give out food."

(65) "Yes, yes. But the old ones, they come here. They do not have to beg. Is there and is free and nobody to pity them. Is almost like shopping." He handed back Ruth Price's photo. "This one, she liked oranges. (70) And sometimes a peach. They do not take more than they need. Is legal?"

"It's okay," she repeated. She didn't tell him that she was glad he put the produce out, glad that Ruth Price got a few oranges (75) every week and had eaten one last night before she died.

Eleanor Taylor Bland, *Slow Burn*.

20. In this excerpt, Ruth Price is
    (1) a customer
    (2) a victim
    (3) a photographer
    (4) a police officer
    (5) a neighbor

21. Which of the following best describes what is happening in this excerpt?
    (1) Joe is trying to sell bad produce to customers.
    (2) The police want Joe to identify some people who have been killed.
    (3) The police are questioning Joe for putting food out for people to take.
    (4) Joe is trying to keep vagrants away from his store.
    (5) A photographer is trying to sell Joe some photographs.

22. Which of the following best describes Joe's behavior toward the "old ones"?
    (1) He tried to help them.
    (2) He wanted to have them arrested.
    (3) He didn't pay any attention to them.
    (4) He was afraid of them.
    (5) He wanted them to find jobs.

Unit 1: Popular Literature

Items 23–28 refer to the following excerpt from a novel.

WHAT ARE THE STAKES IN THIS GAME?

"Come on, Paul," said Finnerty, "I've looked Charley over, and he doesn't look so all-fired bright to me. I've got fifty dollars on you with Goldilocks here, and I'll cover
(5) anybody else who thinks Checker Charley's got a chance."

Eagerly, Shepherd slapped down three twenties. Finnerty covered him.

"Bet the sun won't rise tomorrow,"
(10) said Paul.

"Play," said Finnerty.

Paul settled into his chair again. Dispiritedly, he pushed a checkerpiece forward. One of the youngsters closed
(15) a switch, and a light blinked on, indicating Paul's move on the Checker Charley's bosom, and another light went on, indicating the perfect countermove for Berringer.

Berringer smiled and did what the
(20) machine told him to do. He lit a cigarette and patted the pile of currency beside him.

Paul moved again. A switch was closed, and the lights twinkled appropriately. And so it went for several moves.

(25) To Paul's surprise, he took one of Berringer's pieces without, as far as he could see, laying himself open to any sort of disaster. And then he took another piece, and another. He shook his head in
(30) puzzlement and respect. The machine apparently took a long-range view of the game, with a grand strategy not yet evident. Checker Charley, as though confirming his thoughts, made an ominous
(35) hissing noise, which grew in volume as the game progressed.

Kurt Vonnegut, *Player Piano*.

23. Which phrase best describes Checker Charley?

    (1) a clever player
    (2) an electronic game machine
    (3) Berringer's perfect partner
    (4) a not very bright checkers player
    (5) Finnerty's gambling pal

24. What does Paul mean when he says, "Bet the sun won't rise tomorrow" (line 9)?

    (1) He does not believe the sun will rise.
    (2) He expects to win the game.
    (3) He expects to lose the game.
    (4) He approves of Finnerty's bet.
    (5) He is eager for the game to begin.

25. Why does Berringer pat the pile of money?

    (1) It will make him lucky.
    (2) He believes he will win the money.
    (3) The machine listens to noise at the table.
    (4) The pat closes a switch.
    (5) It acts as a signal to Paul.

26. According to the passage, how is the checkers game turning out?

    (1) Checker Charley is winning.
    (2) Shepherd is losing.
    (3) Berringer is ahead.
    (4) The game is a draw.
    (5) Paul is ahead.

27. Which of the following best describes Finnerty?

    (1) rude
    (2) bored
    (3) confident
    (4) frugal
    (5) cautious

28. Which of the following is the best meaning for "all-fired" (line 3)?

    (1) warmly
    (2) extremely
    (3) flickering
    (4) possibly
    (5) flashy

Items 29–34 are based on the following excerpt from a short story.

WHY DOES THIS MAN CARE SO MUCH?

It was not to be believed and I kept telling myself that, as I walked from the subway station to the high school. And at the same time I couldn't doubt it. I was
(5) scared, scared for Sonny. He became real to me again. A great block of ice got settled in my belly and kept melting there slowly all day long, while I taught my classes algebra. It was a special kind of
(10) ice. It kept melting, sending trickles of ice water all up and down my veins, but it never got less. Sometimes it hardened and seemed to expand until I felt my guts
(15) were going to come spilling out or that I was going to choke or scream. This would always be at a moment when I was remembering some specific thing Sonny had once said or done.
(20) When he was about as old as the boys in my class his face had been bright and open, there was a lot of copper in it; and he'd had wonderfully direct brown eyes, and great gentleness and privacy. I
(25) wondered what he looked like now. He had been picked up, the evening before, in a raid on an apartment downtown, for peddling and using heroin.

James Baldwin, "Sonny's Blues."

29. Which of the following is the best description of the narrator?
    (1) a past friend of Sonny's
    (2) a high school student
    (3) an algebra teacher
    (4) someone Sonny had scared
    (5) Sonny's teacher

30. Which of the following best states the main idea of this passage?
    (1) The narrator is extremely worried about a person he had once known well.
    (2) The narrator uses a chunk of ice to relieve tension.
    (3) The news about Sonny doesn't surprise the narrator at all.
    (4) Boys often get into trouble with the law.
    (5) Drug abuse can touch and hurt many lives.

31. As suggested in this passage, the narrator probably expects Sonny
    (1) to get out of jail because of his charming ways
    (2) to get in even more trouble
    (3) to have changed physically because of drug use
    (4) to be as gentle and direct as before
    (5) to appeal for help in getting a lawyer

32. Why does the author include a long description of the "special kind of ice" (line 9)?
    (1) because it is an effective cure for anxiety
    (2) as a vivid example of how distressed the narrator is
    (3) as a sharp contrast to heartburn
    (4) to show how the digestive system acts under stress
    (5) to suggest the narrator has used too much heroin

33. Which of the following best describes the narrator's feeling about Sonny?
    (1) disgust at what Sonny has become
    (2) fear of Sonny
    (3) relief that Sonny has been caught
    (4) regret for what Sonny once was like
    (5) pleasure that Sonny is no longer around

34. According to the excerpt, the narrator learned of Sonny's arrest
    (1) when he met another teacher on the subway
    (2) after he got to school
    (3) while he was teaching class
    (4) while he was walking into the school building
    (5) before he got to school

Unit 1: Popular Literature 11

Nonfiction

Directions: Choose the best answer to each item.

Items 1–5 refer to the following excerpt from a biography.

HOW CAN HE EVER WIN?

What had changed in America to lead Marshall and his impecunious little band of lawyers to think that they could reverse the tide of segregation in America? How
(5) audacious of this black man and his allies to think they could alter the legal landscape of America!

"I have to keep believing, because I know our cause is right. Justice and
(10) reason are on our side. Everybody knows this but those enslaved to customs that say whites are whites and Negroes are Negroes and never the twain shall meet. But I tell you, it isn't easy knowing that
(15) we'll be going up against the most renowned constitutional lawyer in American history," said Marshall.

Governor Byrnes of South Carolina had pleaded with John William Davis to
(20) argue the South's case for maintaining Jim Crow schools. Byrnes had persuaded Davis to "defend the South" for just a silver tea service—and to satisfy his personal support for "states' rights" and his
(25) conviction that race was just a reality of life that could be reflected in statutes.

While Marshall respected his foe—he had cut classes while in law school to watch the brilliance of Davis's
(30) arguments—he knew that he had a few advantages of his own. He had, in a short period, won thirteen cases before the Supreme Court while losing two. Years earlier, he had enjoyed the heady
(35) compliment of seeing three robed judges of the Fourth Circuit Court of Appeals step off the bench to congratulate him on his successful argument that Virginia had to pay black teachers the same salaries that
(40) it paid white teachers.

I left Marshall that fall day of '53 thinking that he believed in himself and his cause so much that it was impossible for me and others not to believe in him.

Carl T. Rowan, *Dream Makers, Dream Breakers, The World of Justice Thurgood Marshall.*

1. Based on the first paragraph of the excerpt, which statement best describes the writer's belief about the upcoming case?
   (1) The odds favored Marshall.
   (2) The odds were against Marshall.
   (3) Marshall had no chance of winning.
   (4) Marshall was sure to win.
   (5) Both sides had equal chances.

2. When Marshall was congratulated by the three judges, he had argued a case to end
   (1) slavery in America
   (2) segregated schools in the South
   (3) racial inequality for blacks
   (4) unequal pay for black teachers
   (5) states' rights

3. Which of the following best describes Marshall's attitude toward John William Davis?
   (1) contempt
   (2) fear
   (3) anger
   (4) little respect
   (5) great respect

4. What caused the writer to believe in Marshall's chance to win the school segregation case?
   (1) Davis's legal expertise
   (2) Marshall's associates
   (3) Marshall's belief in himself and his cause
   (4) Marshall's success in law school
   (5) the role of Governor Byrnes

5. According to the excerpt, what did Marshall see as one of his advantages?
   (1) He had defeated John William Davis before.
   (2) He had won thirteen cases before the Supreme Court and lost only two.
   (3) He could count on the support of whites throughout the South.
   (4) He had a well-paid staff of lawyers.
   (5) Governor Byrnes was not paying Davis adequately.

Items 6–9 refer to the following excerpt from a biography.

HOW IMPORTANT IS THIS GAME?

Roberto had a tremendous amount of spirit. A few years later, when he was already established in the major leagues, I get a call from the prison in Rio Piedras, (5) inviting me to bring a softball team to play against the inmates. They knew I was a close friend of Roberto's, and since it was the off-season they asked if he could come to play with our team. I said to Roberto, (10) *"Caramba*, they want a softball team to go to the prison to entertain the inmates. Can you come with us on Saturday?"

"Of course. Come pick me up."

At 8:30 in the morning on Saturday I (15) go to his house and he's wearing his Pittsburgh Pirate uniform! As if he were going to a big league game! We went to the prison and everyone was very happy. I was the pitcher for our team—I was slow, (20) and the inmates had a pretty tough bunch. In the first inning they got about five runs off me, I couldn't get a man out! Roberto, who was playing shortstop, comes to the mound and says, *"Que pasa*?" "They're (25) hitting me," I tell him.

"Give me the ball. I don't even like to lose a game in jail," he says.

"But I'm the manager, you can't take me out."

(30) *"Out,"* he says firmly.

He had terrific speed and struck them out one after another. In the fifth inning we were catching up, but we were still a couple runs behind. He came to bat, with (35) two men on base, and I was coaching at third base. He smacks one to right-center field and the ball really takes off. I'm waving the people home and he comes rounding second base. I signal for him to (40) stop but he slides head first into third, and the third baseman goes flying. What a cloud of dust! He gets up, wiping himself off, and I say, "You're *loco*, an expensive big leaguer like you, sliding head first, and (45) look at that poor prisoner over there, he still hasn't gotten up."

"I've always told you I play to win," he says. He was very proud when we won that game.

Kal Wagenheim, *Clemente!*

6. Which of the following best summarizes the main idea of this excerpt?
   (1) Roberto Clemente was a great baseball player.
   (2) Roberto Clemente loved the game of baseball.
   (3) Roberto Clemente always played to win.
   (4) Roberto Clemente enjoyed playing softball.
   (5) Roberto Clemente played prison inmates in softball.

7. Which of the following best describes how well the author knew Clemente?
   (1) He knew Clemente slightly.
   (2) He was a close friend of Clemente.
   (3) He didn't know Clemente at all.
   (4) He was one of Clemente's fans.
   (5) He was Clemente's brother.

8. Which of the following best explains Clemente's wearing his Pittsburgh Pirate's uniform to the softball game?
   (1) He wanted to show off.
   (2) He didn't know it wasn't a regular game.
   (3) He didn't have anything else to wear.
   (4) He took the game seriously.
   (5) He thought it would intimidate the inmates.

9. Based on the excerpt, what word best describes Roberto Clemente?
   (1) intense
   (2) quick-tempered
   (3) selfish
   (4) lazy
   (5) friendly

Unit 1: Popular Literature

Items 10–13 refer to the following excerpt from a magazine article.

WHY IS ROBERT SO PUZZLED?

One summer day, my son Robert, then five years old, took me by the hand and asked me to go outside with him.

Holding on tightly, he carefully walked (5) around the house with me, looking at doors and windows and shaking his head. There was something he didn't understand.

"Mommy," he finally asked, pressing my hand with his warm, chubby fingers, "is our (10) home broken?"

His words shot through my body, altering every protective instinct, activating my private defense system, the one I hold in reserve to ward off attacks against women (15) and children.

"Oh, Robbie," I answered, hugging him, "did someone tell you that we have a broken home?"

"Yes," he said sweetly. "But it doesn't (20) *look* broken!"

"It's not," I assured him. "Our house is not broken and neither are we."

I explained that "broken" is some people's way of describing a home with (25) only one parent, usually the mother. Sometimes there was only one parent because of divorce, like us. "There are still lots of homes like ours. And they're still homes."

(30) Robbie looked relieved and went to play with his friends. I stood there, shaking with anger.

What a way to put down a little kid and me, too, I thought. I supported my (35) three children, fed and clothed them. I was there for them emotionally and physically. I managed to keep up payments on the house. Although we struggled financially, we were happy and loving. What was (40) "broken" about us?

Carol Kleiman, "My Home Is Not Broken, It Works."

10. When Robert asks if his home is broken, to what is he referring?
    (1) his house
    (2) his mother and father
    (3) his mother and himself
    (4) women and children
    (5) his divorced mother

11. According to this excerpt, which of the following is the best meaning for the phrase "to ward off" (line 14)?
    (1) to run away from
    (2) to object to
    (3) to defend against
    (4) to put a curse on
    (5) to accept

12. Which of the following pairs of words would best describe an important contrast between Robert and his mother as demonstrated in the passage?
    (1) whole and broken
    (2) innocent and experienced
    (3) sad and productive
    (4) angry and supportive
    (5) relieved and loving

13. Which of the following best summarizes the main idea of this excerpt?
    (1) that children are curious
    (2) that a carelessly spoken word can cause harm
    (3) how quickly children can recover from hurt
    (4) how adults can become angry over unimportant issues
    (5) that divorce makes a person overly sensitive

Items 14–17 refer to the following excerpt from a book.

WHAT WASN'T OBVIOUS TO THE AUDIENCE?

Early in this century, a horse named Hans amazed the people of Berlin by his extraordinary ability to perform rapid calculations in mathematics. After a
(5) problem was written on a blackboard placed in front of him, he promptly counted out the answer by tapping the low numbers with his right forefoot and multiples of ten with his left. Trickery was
(10) ruled out because Hans's owner, unlike other owners of other performing animals, did not profit financially—and Hans even performed his feats whether or not the owner was present. The psychologist
(15) O. Pfungst witnessed one of these performances and became convinced that there had to be a more logical explanation than the uncanny intelligence of a horse.

Because Hans performed only in the
(20) presence of an audience that could see the blackboard and therefore knew the correct answer, Pfungst reasoned that the secret lay in observation of the audience rather than the horse. He finally
(25) discovered that as soon as the problem was written on the blackboard, the audience bent forward very slightly in anticipation to watch Hans's forefeet. As slight as that movement was, Hans
(30) perceived it and took it as his signal to begin tapping. As his taps approached the correct number, the audience became tense with excitement and made almost imperceptible movements of the head
(35) which signaled Hans to stop counting. The audience, simply by expecting Hans to stop when the correct number was reached, had actually told the animal when to stop. Pfungst clearly demonstrated
(40) that Hans's intelligence was nothing but a mechanical response to his audience, which unwittingly communicated the answer by its body language.

Peter Farb, *Word Play: What Happens When People Talk.*

14. Why was Hans's performance considered amazing by his audience?
    (1) Horses usually can't do math problems.
    (2) Hans was faster than the average horse.
    (3) Hans's owner didn't make a profit.
    (4) Hans obviously enjoyed his unusual work.
    (5) The audience couldn't figure out the trick involved.

15. Which of the following statements is the most important about what Pfungst concluded regarding Hans's performance?
    (1) Hans wasn't really a math genius.
    (2) The performance had to be in front of an audience.
    (3) The audience already knew the answer.
    (4) Hans's response was mechanical.
    (5) Body language can communicate expectations.

16. If Hans were a man instead of a horse, he could have enhanced his act by
    (1) adding a few magic tricks
    (2) doing calculus problems
    (3) removing the blackboard
    (4) paying even closer attention to the audience
    (5) wearing a blindfold

17. Why does the author use the words logical (line 17) and reasoned (line 22) in connection with psychologist Pfungst?
    (1) to make him seem more intelligent than the audience
    (2) to emphasize the scientific validity of the discovery
    (3) because they contrast with body language
    (4) because they are the basis of spoken language
    (5) to explain why Pfungst wanted to understand the secret

Unit 1: Popular Literature

Items 18–22 refer to the following excerpt from a newspaper column.

WHAT IS THE FUTURE FOR THE CHILDREN?

It is not surprising that modern children tend to look blank and dispirited when informed that they will someday have to "go to work and make a living." The
(5) problem is that they cannot visualize what work is in corporate America.

Not so long ago, when a parent said he was off to work, the child knew very well what was about to happen. His parent was
(10) going to make something or fix something. The parent could take his offspring to his place of business and let him watch while he repaired a buggy or built a table.

When a child asked, "What kind of
(15) work do you do, Daddy?" his father could answer in terms that a child could come to grips with. "I fix steam engines." "I make horse collars."

Well, a few fathers still fix engines and
(20) build things, but most do not. Nowadays, most fathers sit in glass buildings performing tasks that are absolutely incomprehensible to children. The answers they give when asked, "What
(25) kind of work do you do, Daddy?" are likely to be utterly mystifying to a child.

"I sell space." "I do market research." "I am a data processor." "I am in public relations." "I am a systems analyst." Such
(30) explanations must seem nonsense to a child. How can he possibly envision anyone analyzing a system or researching a market?

Russell Baker, "Poor Russell"s Almanac."

18. Which of the following does not explain why "modern children tend to look blank and dispirited" (lines 1–2)?
    (1) They cannot mentally picture what work is.
    (2) Modern work often may not look like anything.
    (3) A child often cannot watch the work being done.
    (4) Children don't want to earn their own livings.
    (5) Modern job titles may not make sense to children.

19. To what effect did the author use the word envision (line 31) in the last sentence?
    (1) as evidence that no one can see a system
    (2) to bring the reader back to the idea in the first paragraph
    (3) to emphasize how incomprehensible modern jobs are
    (4) to contrast with the idea of nonsense
    (5) to suggest that we must look to the future

20. Which of the following best states an assumption the author displays in the article?
    (1) In most families, only the father works.
    (2) Most children today are lazy.
    (3) Old jobs were better because everyone knew what they were.
    (4) Father's shouldn't work if their children don't know what they do.
    (5) Today's jobs are unsatisfactory.

21. The author's main purpose in writing the article is to
    (1) give facts about jobs
    (2) state an opinion about jobs
    (3) pose questions about work
    (4) give statistics about work
    (5) provide results of opinion polls

22. According to the excerpt, the author believes that the nature of work has become too
    (1) impersonal
    (2) visual
    (3) time consuming
    (4) concrete
    (5) abstract

Items 23–28 refer to the following excerpt from a book.

WHY IS SNOWBIRD MEMORABLE?

Snowbird (he never uses any other name; everyone in his world knows who he is) came to town reluctantly that winter. His wife was ill. Physically, he stood about
(5) five feet tall in his caribou-skin boots. His hands were dark and wide, the skin thick like leather, showing, as I remember my grandfather's hands had shown, the collected strength and scars of many
(10) years in the open. Snowbird's face, heavily lined, was free of expression as it peered from under the peak of a battered baseball cap. It was a sport he had never heard of. But the old eyes, even behind bifocals,
(15) were sharp and clear. Snowbird has lived in the Canadian bush, in cabins, behind lean-tos, on mattresses of boughs, and under buffalo robe blankets and the crisp stars ever since Theodore Roosevelt was
(20) President of the United States. Snowbird is unable to read words on paper. But he can read tracks and blood in the snow and branches broken certain ways, and sounds in the air. He knows the colors of
(25) good clouds and bad clouds and the sunsets and different winds that presage tomorrow's weather. He knows tales as timeless as their morals. He has some theories on modern problems. And he can
(30) speak four languages—Cree, English, Chipewyan, and dog—sometimes in the same sentence. "I'm seventy-seven years old," he told us. "I'm just beginning to grow."

Andrew H. Malcolm, *The Canadians*

23. How can Snowbird's life before he came to the town be best described?

    (1) tragic
    (2) rough
    (3) carefree
    (4) stressful
    (5) uneventful

24. Which of the following best describes how the author feels about Snowbird?

    (1) awed
    (2) fascinated
    (3) pitying
    (4) confused
    (5) sad

25. Although Snowbird cannot "read words on paper" (line 21), he is able to

    (1) read the feelings in a person's heart
    (2) read old tales
    (3) read the sights and sounds of nature
    (4) remember Theodore Roosevelt
    (5) teach four languages

26. Why does the author conclude this paragraph with a quotation from Snowbird himself?

    (1) to prove that he did know Snowbird
    (2) as evidence of Snowbird's age
    (3) as an example of Snowbird's knowledge of languages
    (4) to sum up Snowbird's world view
    (5) as evidence of Snowbird's knowledge of nature

27. According to the excerpt, Snowbird is

    (1) young
    (2) tall
    (3) short
    (4) pale
    (5) fat

28. Which of the following best summarizes Snowbird's attitude toward his life?

    (1) He is eager to continue living and learning.
    (2) He feels he has learned all he needs to know.
    (3) He has become bored with life.
    (4) He thinks he is too old to go on.
    (5) He just wants to take it easy.

Unit 1: Popular Literature

Poetry

Directions: Choose the best answer to each item.

Items 1–4 refer to the following poem.

WHAT IS REALLY GOING ON?

Splitting Wood at Six Above

I open a tree.
In the stupefying cold
—ice on bare flesh a scald—
I seat the metal wedge
(5) with a few left-handed swipes,
then with a change of grips
lean into the eight-pound sledge.

It's muslin overhead.
Snow falls as heavy as salt.
(10) You are four months dead.
The beech log comes apart
like a chocolate nougat.
The wood speaks
first in the tiny voice
(15) of a bird cry, a puppet-squeak,
and then all in a rush,
all in a passionate stammer.
The papery soul of the beech
released by wedge and hammer
(20) flies back into air.

Time will do this as fair
to hickory, birch, black oak,
easing the insects in
till rot and freeze combine
(25) to raise out wormwood cracks,
blue and dainty, the souls.
They are thin as an eyelash.
They flap once going up.

The air rings like a bell.
(30) I breathe out drops—
cold morning ghost-puffs
like your old cigarette cough.
See you tomorrow, you said.
You lied.
(35) We're far from finished! I'm still
talking to you (last night's dream);
we'll split the phone bill.
It's expensive calling
from the other side.

(40) Even waking it seems
logical—
your small round
stubbornly airborne soul,
that sun-yellow daisy heart
(45) slipping the noose of its pod,
scooting over the tightrope,
none the worse for its trip,
to arrive at the other side.

It is the sound
(50) of your going I drive
into heartwood. I stack
my quartered cuts bark down,
open yellow-face up.

Maxine Kumin, *Our Ground Time Here Will Be Brief.*

1. The overall emotion expressed in the poem is

   (1) rage
   (2) relief
   (3) intensity
   (4) grief
   (5) fatigue

2. The lines, "I stack / my quartered cuts bark down, / open yellow-face up." (lines 51–53), are a comparison to the speaker's

   (1) departed loved one
   (2) own feelings that are still raw
   (3) hands that are raw from splitting wood
   (4) skin that is chapped from the cold
   (5) other stacks of wood

3. In lines 11–12, the speaker compares cutting into a beech log to

   (1) cutting down an oak tree
   (2) snow as heavy as salt
   (3) ice on bare flesh
   (4) dying
   (5) biting into a piece of candy

4. The "you" addressed by the speaker in the poem is

   (1) a stranger
   (2) a loved one
   (3) a distant relative
   (4) a child
   (5) an enemy

Unit 1: Popular Literature

Items 5–8 refer to the following poem.

WHAT HAPPENS AS THE CHILD SLEEPS?
A Poem for Emily

Small fact and fingers and farthest one from me,
a hand's width and two generations away,
in this still present I am fifty-three.
You are not yet a full day.

(5) When I am sixty-three, when you are ten,
and you are neither closer nor as far,
your arms will fill with what you know by then,
the arithmetic and love we do and are.

When I by blood and luck am eighty-six
(10) and you are some place else and thirty-three
believing in sex and god and politics
with children who look not at all like me,

some time I know you will have read them this
so they will know I love them and say so
(15) and love their mother. Child, whatever is
is always or never was. Long ago,

a day I watched a while beside your bed,
I wrote this down, a thing that might be kept
a while, to tell you what I would have said
(20) when you were who knows what and I was dead
which is I stood and loved you while you slept.

Miller Williams, "A Poem for Emily."

5. Which of the following best characterizes the situation in this poem?
   (1) a mother speaking to her newborn daughter
   (2) a father writing to his baby son
   (3) a man speaking to his newborn grandson
   (4) a man writing to his newborn granddaughter
   (5) a man writing to his three-year-old daughter

6. How old is the speaker in this poem?
   (1) thirty-three
   (2) fifty-three
   (3) sixty-three
   (4) eighty-six
   (5) none of the above

7. What is the best summary of the message the speaker wants to convey?
   (1) Time passes all too quickly.
   (2) Children should love their parents.
   (3) Love endures.
   (4) Children's beliefs change as they grow up.
   (5) The future is unpredictable.

8. The speaker expects Emily's children to
   (1) look like the speaker
   (2) know nothing of the speaker
   (3) know about this poem
   (4) go into politics
   (5) feel unloved

Items 9–14 refer to the following poem.

HOW DOES THIS HOUSE GET WARM?
Those Winter Sundays

Sundays too my father got up early
and put his clothes on in the blueblack cold,
then with crackled hands that ached
from labor in the weekday weather made
(5) banked fires blaze. No one ever thanked him.

I'd wake and hear the cold splintering, breaking.
When the rooms were warm, he'd call,
and slowly I would rise and dress,
fearing the chronic angers of that house.

(10) Speaking indifferently to him,
who had driven out the cold
and polished my good shoes as well.
What did I know, what did I know
of love's austere and lonely offices?

Robert Hayden, "Those Winter Sundays."

9. Which of the following statements about the father's work cannot be inferred from the poem?
   (1) His job began early in the morning.
   (2) He worked outdoors.
   (3) He worked on weekdays.
   (4) His work required hard labor.
   (5) He didn't like his work.

10. Which of the following sets of images is the most important to the main idea of the poem?
    (1) night and day
    (2) waking and sleeping
    (3) warmth and cold
    (4) old clothes and good shoes
    (5) indifference and anger

11. In the context of this poem, what does the poet mean by "love's austere and lonely offices" (line 14)?
    (1) the son's attitude toward the father
    (2) the father's dutiful care of the family
    (3) the angers that woke the house
    (4) the father's attitude toward the weather
    (5) rising and dressing alone

12. What is the poet's attitude toward his own past behavior?
    (1) He is satisfied with his childhood behavior.
    (2) He believes he was right to be angry.
    (3) He thinks that teenage indifference is normal.
    (4) He regrets his thoughtless lack of understanding.
    (5) He thinks he loved his father too much.

13. Which of the following is the best way to describe the meaning of "I'd wake and hear the cold splintering, breaking." (line 6)?
    (1) the windows were shattering
    (2) the fire was warming the rooms
    (3) icicles were forming
    (4) glass was breaking
    (5) the pipes were freezing and breaking

14. Which of the following can be inferred from the poem?
    (1) The boy would go to church.
    (2) The boy would go to school.
    (3) The father would go to work.
    (4) The father would go back to bed.
    (5) The boy would go to the office with his father.

Unit 1: Popular Literature

Items 15–20 refer to the following poem.

WHY IS THE MOMENT IMPORTANT?
That Moment

When the pistol muzzle oozing blue vapour
Was lifted away
Like a cigarette lifted from an ashtray

And the only face left in the world
(5) Lay broken
Between hands that relaxed, being too late

And the trees closed forever
And the streets closed forever

And the body lay on the gravel
(10) Of the abandoned world
Among abandoned utilities
Exposed to infinity forever

Crow had to start searching for something to eat.

Ted Hughes, "That Moment."

15. What is the situation described in this poem?
    (1) A bird is waiting for a man to die.
    (2) A man has been shot on a country road.
    (3) A person has been shot in the city.
    (4) A man has died in a nuclear explosion.
    (5) The end of the world has come.

16. What is the effect of the phrase "like a cigarette lifted from an ashtray" (line 3)?
    (1) It implies a casualness to the killing.
    (2) It reveals that the killer smoked.
    (3) The reader visualizes the smoke.
    (4) The reader is brought closer to the violence.
    (5) It leads to the image of a face.

17. In what way does the poet emphasize the finality of death?
    (1) by stating the hands were relaxed
    (2) with the image of the Crow
    (3) by repeating several key words
    (4) with the word exposed (line 12)
    (5) by using only one sentence for the poem

18. What would Crow probably do when told his wife was pregnant?
    (1) be overjoyed
    (2) start crying
    (3) get angry
    (4) get a second job
    (5) become depressed

19. To whom do the "hands that relaxed, being too late" (line 6) belong?
    (1) the speaker
    (2) the person who was killed
    (3) an unknown assailant
    (4) the killer who was caught
    (5) Crow

20. Which of the following sayings best summarizes the meaning of the last line of the poem?
    (1) Revenge is sweet.
    (2) Life must go on.
    (3) Hunger is a basic instinct.
    (4) Only the fit survive.
    (5) Hope springs eternal.

Items 21–26 refer to the following poem.

WHAT IS THIS OLD COUPLE DOING?

The Bean Eaters

They eat beans mostly, this old yellow pair.
Dinner is a casual affair.
Plain chipware on a plain and creaking wood,
Tin flatware.

(5) Two who are Mostly Good.
Two who have lived their day,
But keep on putting on their clothes
And putting things away.

And remembering…
(10) Remembering, with twinklings and twinges,
As they lean over the beans in their rented back room
   that is full of beads and receipts and dolls and cloths,
   tobacco crumbs, vases and fringes.

Gwendolyn Brooks, "The Bean Eaters."

21. What does the poet mean by "a plain and creaking wood" (line 3)?

    (1) an old pine floor
    (2) a used board
    (3) a bare old table
    (4) an old squeaky door
    (5) a refinished antique

22. According to the description in this poem, the couple will probably

    (1) go on welfare
    (2) die poor and miserable
    (3) get tired of beans
    (4) long for better days
    (5) die poor but happy

23. Which of the following would best explain why the poet wrote an extra line in the last stanza?

    (1) to break the monotony of the rhyme scheme
    (2) as evidence of departing from convention
    (3) to show the wealth of the couple's memories
    (4) as evidence of the poverty of the couple's home
    (5) to explain what things have been put away

24. Why are the words Mostly Good (line 5) capitalized?

    (1) to follow the rules of grammar
    (2) as evidence of the couple's way of life
    (3) to suggest that the people are not really good
    (4) to suggest that the two are saintlike
    (5) to emphasize how tidy the couple is

25. Which of the following best describes the couple in the poem?

    (1) They are looking forward to death.
    (2) They are very neat and orderly.
    (3) They are surrounded by reminders of their lives.
    (4) They have a comfortable retirement.
    (5) Their house is too small.

26. What is the best interpretation of "Remembering, with twinkling and twinges" (line 10)?

    (1) The couple can't remember their past.
    (2) They remember both good and bad times.
    (3) They finally remembered where they put all their old things.
    (4) They wish they could remember where they put all their old things.
    (5) They wish they were young again.

Unit 1: Popular Literature

Items 27–32 refer to the following poem.

WHY IS SHE PAINTING THE GATE?
Painting the Gate

    I painted the mailbox. That was fun.
    I painted it postal blue.
    Then I painted the gate.
    I painted a spider that got on the gate.
(5) I painted his mate.
    I painted the ivy around the gate.
    Some stones I painted blue,
    and part of the cat as he rubbed by.
    I painted my hair. I painted my shoe.
(10) I painted the slats, both front and back,
    all their beveled edges, too.
    I painted the numbers on the gate—
    I shouldn't have, but it was too late.
    I painted the posts, each side and top.
(15) I painted the hinges, the handle, the lock,
    several ants and a moth asleep in a crack.
    At last I was through.
    I'd painted the gate
    shut, me out, with both hands dark blue,
(20) as well as my nose, which,
    early on, because of a sudden itch,
    got painted. But wait!
    I had painted the gate.

May Swenson, "Painting the Gate."

27. The "numbers on the gate" (line 12) refer to
    (1) graffiti
    (2) operating instructions
    (3) a model number
    (4) a street address
    (5) a ZIP Code

28. What got painted "because of a sudden itch"?
    (1) her hands
    (2) her nose
    (3) the gate
    (4) the hinges
    (5) a moth

29. Which of the following objects that the speaker painted is least essential to the effect of the poem?
    (1) the spider
    (2) her shoe
    (3) the numbers on the gate
    (4) the posts
    (5) the locks

30. How was the poet probably feeling when she wrote this poem?
    (1) serious
    (2) unhappy
    (3) lighthearted
    (4) ambitious
    (5) contented

31. Why did the speaker in this poem paint her mailbox "postal blue"?
    (1) That was the only color she had.
    (2) Blue was the color of the gate.
    (3) Blue is the color associated with the post office.
    (4) Blue is a popular color.
    (5) It suited her mood.

32. If the speaker in this poem decided to cook for two of her friends, she would probably
    (1) serve a gourmet meal
    (2) make enough for ten people
    (3) measure exact portions
    (4) paint the kitchen first
    (5) mail invitations to them

Unit 1: Popular Literature

Items 33–36 refer to the following excerpt from a poem.

WHERE IS LISA?
Lisa

Under the great down-curving lilac branches
a dome of coolness and a cave of bloom,
Lisa, vague-eyed, chin-propped, cross-legged, is sitting
within a leaf-walled room.

(5) Beyond the curtaining green,
      her brothers wrangle,
cars pass, a huckster shouts, a bicycle bell
is brisk, is brief, dogs bark.
      She does not hear them.
(10) She is netted in silence, she is lost in a spell.

Constance Carrier, "Lisa."

33. Which of the following would be the best alternative title to this poem?

    (1) A Refuge for a Child
    (2) Running from Her Brothers
    (3) Love of Nature
    (4) The Deaf Child
    (5) Instructions for Sulking

34. According to this excerpt, the emotional state Lisa is in would probably be most similar to that of

    (1) a woman going to a bar
    (2) an artist working in her studio
    (3) a musician practicing with her band
    (4) a lawyer presenting evidence to the jury
    (5) a novice nun in a convent

35. In the poem, Lisa is sitting

    (1) in a cave
    (2) under a bush
    (3) beneath a dome
    (4) in a room
    (5) on a branch

36. It can be inferred from the poem that Lisa is alone because

    (1) her brothers won't let her play with them
    (2) she is afraid of the dogs
    (3) she can't ride a bicycle
    (4) she likes to think and dream
    (5) she is lost

Items 37–39 refer to the following poem.

HOW DOES THE SKY CHANGE?

How to Write a Poem About the Sky
For the students of the Bethel
Middle School, Bethel, Alaska—Feb. 1975

      You see the sky now
(5) colder than the frozen river
      so dense and white
      little birds
      walk across it.

      You see the sky now
(10) but the earth
      is lost in it
      and there are no horizons.
      It is all
      a single breath.

(15) You see the sky
      but the earth is called
      by the same name
         the moment
         the wind shifts
(20) sun splits it open
      and bluish membranes
      push through slits of skin.

      You see the sky.

Leslie Marmon Silko, *Storyteller*.

37. The "bluish membranes" (line 21) refer to
    (1) the river
    (2) the snow
    (3) the sky
    (4) the wind
    (5) the earth

38. Which of the following best explains the repeated use of the phrase, "You see the sky"?
    (1) It is hard to see the sky in winter.
    (2) You need to have good eyesight to write a poem.
    (3) Each time you look at the sky, it is different.
    (4) The sky is the same as a frozen river.
    (5) Time seems to stop when you look at the winter sky for a long time.

39. It can be inferred from the poem that the speaker
    (1) works to save the environment
    (2) does not like the cold
    (3) is a student
    (4) is inspired by nature
    (5) lives in Alaska

Items 40–42 refer to the following poem.

IS THIS PERSON BRAVE?

Life Doesn't Frighten Me at All

Shadows on the wall
Noises down the hall
Life doesn't frighten me at all
Bad dogs barking loud
(5) Big ghosts in a cloud
Life doesn't frighten me at all.

Mean old Mother Goose
Lions on the loose
They don't frighten me at all
(10) Dragons breathing flame
On my counterpane
That doesn't frighten me at all.

I go boo
Make them shoo
(15) I make fun
Way they run
I won't cry
So they fly
I just smile
(20) They go wild
Life doesn't frighten me at all.

Tough guys in a fight
All alone at night
Life doesn't frighten me at all.
(25) Panthers in the park
Strangers in the dark
No, they don't frighten me at all.
That new classroom where
Boys all pull my hair
(30) (Kissy little girls
With their hair in curls)
They don't frighten me at all.

Don't show me frogs and snakes
And listen for my screams,
(35) If I'm afraid at all
It's only in my dreams.

I've got a magic charm
That I keep up my sleeve,
I can walk the ocean floor
(40) And never have to breathe.

Life doesn't frighten me at all
Not at all
Not at all.
Life doesn't frighten me at all.

Maya Angelou, *The Complete Collected Poems of Maya Angelou.*

40. Which of the following is the speaker afraid of?

   (1) shadows
   (2) ghosts
   (3) bad dogs
   (4) frogs
   (5) strangers

41. What is the effect of repeating the line "Life doesn't frighten me at all"?

   (1) to show that the speaker is trying to sound brave
   (2) to show that the speaker brags
   (3) to show that the speaker repeats herself
   (4) to make the reader impatient
   (5) to make the reader afraid

42. Which of the following best describes the speaker in the poem?

   (1) an adult
   (2) a young girl
   (3) a small child
   (4) a teenager
   (5) an older man

Drama

Directions: Choose the best answer to each item.

Items 1–3 refer to the following excerpt from a play.

HAS IT BEEN THAT LONG?

MAGGIE: Well, you never know.
MAGGY: No, you never really do. *(Pause.)* You know what? I was a little scared, meeting you again after all these years.
(5) MAGGIE: You were? So was I.
MAGGY: Why were you scared?
MAGGIE: I was afraid it would be awkward and horrible. That our faces would all hurt from fake smiling.
(10) MAGGY: Oh, I hate that.
MAGGIE: Why were you scared?
MAGGY: Because I felt guilty.
MAGGIE: Guilty?
MAGGY: About being the one who got Jim.
(15) Sometimes I worry that I got him under false pretenses.
MAGGIE: What do you mean?
MAGGY: I almost told you about this the other night. Jim and I met at a Fourth
(20) of July parade, did he tell you that?
MAGGIE: Uh-huh.
MAGGY: He was standing there watching the floats, and I kind of sidled over and stood next to him. I remembered him
(25) from school. In fact, I remembered him as your boyfriend. It was surprising to see him standing there by himself all those years later, looking sort of lost and lonely. I just assumed he'd married
(30) you and gone off to become a big shot somewhere—you know, Brown Book Award and all.
MAGGIE: *(Smiling.)* Yeah.
MAGGY: Anyway, there I stood next to Jim
(35) looking at the parade, feeling kind of stupid, and here's what I thought: "If I were Maggie Mulroney right now, what would I say?"
MAGGIE: Uh-oh.
(40) MAGGY: And at that moment a float went by with Gina Lazlo on it. She was looking a little the worse for wear—to tell you the truth she kind of peaked in 12th grade. She was all dolled up as some kind of
(45) overweight sex goddess on a float that said Bigelow Pontiac—she married Robbie Bigelow, did you know that?
MAGGIE: No!
MAGGY: Yes! So here she is on Robbie's
(50) float waving a wand, you really had to be there to appreciate the full impact, and I said, "Living proof. You drive 'em off the lot, and they lose their value instantly." *(Maggie laughs.)* Hey, it was
(55) a start.
MAGGIE: I like it.
MAGGY: Yeah, so did he. He looked at me like I'd just arrived on the Planet, one of those "what have we here?" looks,
(60) you know?
MAGGIE: Yeah.
MAGGY: And I felt like a million dollars. Suddenly, with my new personality, I felt so free and liberated. It was great.
(65) But after a while I started to worry. I said to myself, "This isn't really you. Who is it?" Of course I knew the answer right away. It was you.

Catherine Butterfield, *Joined at the Head.*

1. The two women having this conversation

   (1) know little about one another
   (2) are old friends
   (3) have never met before
   (4) have recently met
   (5) wish they were somewhere else

2. Which of the following best summarizes Maggy's thoughts about Gina Lazlo?

   (1) She is envious of Gina's looks.
   (2) She is jealous of Gina's marriage to Robbie Bigelow.
   (3) She thinks Gina looks foolish.
   (4) She thinks Gina's looks have improved since high school.
   (5) She likes Gina better than she likes Maggie.

3. When Maggy visits with other friends she probably

   (1) has trouble thinking of something to say
   (2) doesn't gossip
   (3) listens a lot
   (4) talks a lot
   (5) prefers to be doing something else

Unit 1: Popular Literature 27

Items 4–7 refer to the following excerpt from a play.

DOES BING REALLY GO FROM A TO Z?

LEANARA: Recite my favorite part. Right from the playwright's mouth.

BING: "I ran down into the subway. In a panic. I'll go anywhere. Trains rush (5) past me. E trains. F trains. A's. GG's. RR's. C's. Pursued by the entire alphabet."

LEANARA: I love it. I love you. Are you in as much pain as the play says?

(10) BING: Oh, yes. More.

LEANARA: How do you stand it? How do you live?

BING: Well, no, not really. You see I make up bad things about myself so I'll be (15) more interesting. I read about O'Neill and I think I could have been a great playwright too if my Mother was a junkie and my father was a miser who ran around playing the Count of Monte (20) Cristo all the time. So I write my autobiographical play, based on Dante's *Inferno*, and it's close enough to the way I'd like my life to be. With a few songs thrown in. Oh, God!

(25) LEANARA: What is it?

BING: *(Pulls a small box out of his shopping bag.)* I bought these cufflinks at a little magic store on Fourteenth Street. One has the initial R and the other set has (30) the initial F. I mix them up and wear them R and F. For rich and famous. Sometimes I wear them the other way around. For famous and rich. I don't care which one comes first. But if my (35) play stinks. If my play flops. I'm going to be wearing them D & B. For dead and buried. O & O. For over and out. I'm not going to be the World's Oldest Living Promising Young Playwright.

John Guare, *Rich and Famous*.

4. Bing makes himself seem more interesting by
   (1) taking a lot of subway trains
   (2) practicing magic
   (3) pretending he is like the man in his play
   (4) imitating details of O'Neill's life
   (5) reciting the entire alphabet

5. If Bing's play is a success, which of the following might he have engraved on a tie clasp?
   (1) O & O
   (2) D & B
   (3) W O L P Y P
   (4) A O K
   (5) A W O L

6. In this scene, the author probably intends Bing to seem
   (1) confident
   (2) very young
   (3) successful
   (4) middle-aged
   (5) in love

7. Which of the following is the best reason for the author having Bing mention O'Neill?
   (1) to show how much Bing knows about theater history
   (2) because the author likes O'Neill
   (3) to show how little Bing really understands about greatness
   (4) because Bing's father was a miser too
   (5) to explain why the *Inferno* was a success

Items 8–13 refer to the following excerpt from a play.

CAN RITA GET A TUTOR?

FRANK: I'll make a bargain with you. Yes? I'll tell you everything I know—but if I do that you must promise never to come back here. You see I never—I (5) didn't actually want to take this course in the first place. I allowed myself to be talked into it. I knew it was wrong. Seeing you only confirms my suspicion. My dear, it's not your fault, just the luck (10) of the draw that you got me; but get me you did. And the thing is, between you, me and the walls, I'm actually an appalling teacher. *(After a pause.)* Most of the time, you see, it doesn't (15) actually matter—appalling teaching is quite in order for most appalling students. And the others manage to get by despite me. But you're different. You want a lot, and I can't give it. *(He* (20) *moves towards her.)* Everything I know—and you must listen to this—is that I know absolutely nothing. I don't like the hours, you know. *(He goes to the swivel chair and sits.)* Strange (25) hours for the Open University thing. They expect us to teach when the pubs are open. I can be a good teacher when I'm in the pub, you know. Four pints of weak Guinness and I can be (30) as witty as Wilde. I'm sorry—there are other tutors—I'll arrange it for you...post it on...*(He looks at her.)* *(RITA slowly turns and goes out and quietly closes the door behind her. Suddenly* (35) *the door bursts open and RITA flies in.)*

RITA *(going up to him)* Wait a minute, listen to me. Listen: I'm on this course, you are my teacher—an' you're gonna bleedin' well teach me.

(40) FRANK: There are other tutors—I've told you...

RITA: You're my tutor. I don't want another tutor.

Willie Russell, *Educating Rita.*

8. Why doesn't Frank want to teach Rita?
   (1) He doesn't want to see her again.
   (2) He doesn't believe he is a very good teacher.
   (3) He has too many students already.
   (4) She's too argumentative for him.
   (5) They know each other too well.

9. With which of the following proverbs would Frank be most likely to agree?
   (1) Don't let the grass grow under your feet.
   (2) Rome was not built in a day.
   (3) Time is money.
   (4) You can't make a silk purse out of a sow's ear.
   (5) He who hesitates is lost.

10. What is the effect of Rita's leaving quietly, then flying back in?
    (1) It makes Frank angry.
    (2) It indicates that Rita has changed her mind.
    (3) It shows how important Frank really is.
    (4) It provides a use for the door in the set.
    (5) It shows how confused Rita is.

11. Which of the following attitudes is suggested by Frank's long, rambling speech?
    (1) uncertainty
    (2) sternness
    (3) affection
    (4) friendliness
    (5) hostility

12. Why does Frank think he is a terrible teacher?
    (1) He likes the hours.
    (2) He holds classes in the local pub.
    (3) He is very witty.
    (4) He thinks he knows absolutely nothing.
    (5) His students are appalling.

13. Which of the following best summarizes the reason Rita gives for Frank to be her tutor?
    (1) She enjoys his classes.
    (2) There are no other tutors.
    (3) No one was assigned as her tutor.
    (4) He was assigned as her tutor.
    (5) She has heard how good he is.

Items 14–17 refer to the following excerpt from a play.

WHY DOES THIS PRIEST HAVE TO LEAVE?

O'MALLEY: *(coming forward, sitting down on a sawhorse)* Father, I won't be here at Christmas. *(It takes the old man a moment to grasp the significance* (5) *of this.)*

FITZGIBBON: Huh?

O'MALLEY: Well, I was with the Bishop this afternoon and he's transferring me to another parish.

(10) FITZGIBBON: *(coming forward to him, in great alarm)* Oh, you're leaving me? Why, now it never occurred to me that some day you might. But, me boy, what am I going to do without you? (15) You didn't ask to go?

O'MALLEY: *(smiling)* Oh, no, no, father! As a matter of fact, I asked to stay with you, but *(a little embarrassed)* the Bishop asked me to help him out and I—

(20) FITZGIBBON: *(worried)* But St. Dominic's— what's going to happen?

O'MALLEY: *(calmingly)* Oh, you'll be all right, Father. I wish you could have heard some of the things the Bishop said (25) about you—it would have done you good. He says you're looking ten years younger. He has all the confidence in the world in you. Now, don't worry, you'll have a new assistant. *(Fitzgibbon* (30) *comes around the sawhorse and sits down by O'Malley.)*

FITZGIBBON: Well, now, I want to wish you all the success in the world, which I know you'll have. *(Hopefully)* Is it a (35) parish of your own?

O'MALLEY: Well, no, not—not exactly, Father. You see, this—this church, St. Charles, it's —uh—well, the pastor is getting along in years and things (40) aren't—

FITZGIBBON: *(cocking his head at him)* You mean they're in trouble?

O'MALLEY: Yes. And I'm supposed to go in there and try and help them.

(45) FITZGIBBON: You mean without the old fellow knowing it?

O'MALLEY: *(smiling)* Uh-huh.

FITZGIBBON: *(innocently, reassuring O'Malley)* Well, now that's a difficult (50) assignment. But it'll work out. You may have trouble with the old man at first. He may be runnin' off to the Bishop every few minutes, but don't let that bother you. Ah, you'll bring him around to your way (55) of thinkin'.

Frank Butler and Frank Cavett, *Going My Way*.

14. The "St. Dominic's" (line 20) Fitzgibbon refers to is probably a
    (1) small town
    (2) school
    (3) city
    (4) church parish
    (5) priest

15. If O'Malley were a computer scientist, which of the following would he probably be employed as?
    (1) a software troubleshooter
    (2) a researcher
    (3) a hardware developer
    (4) a marketing expert
    (5) a program designer

16. Most of the stage directions in this passage are intended to
    (1) show how friendly these men are
    (2) show how Father Fitzgibbon is getting old
    (3) indicate the tension between the two men
    (4) define O'Malley's personality
    (5) suggest secrecy

17. The final stage direction for Father Fitzgibbon (lines 48–49) is used to suggest that
    (1) he is simpleminded
    (2) he is actually describing his own earlier behavior
    (3) O'Malley is very much in need of assurance
    (4) he still doesn't understand what is going on
    (5) he is still a quite competent pastor

Items 18–23 refer to the following excerpt from a play.

WHO WAS MARY, ANYWAY?

TIFFANY: *(rising, too, pursuing the subject)* Did you kiss her that night?

BOB: Come on, put on your coat. You're just stalling for time.

(5) TIFFANY: I'll bet you did.

BOB: What?

TIFFANY: Kiss her that night.

BOB: I didn't kiss her for weeks.

TIFFANY: I don't believe it. You kissed me on (10) the second night—in the elevator—do you remember?

BOB: *(thinking of* MARY*)* Oh, I made certain fumbling attempts—but she'd make some little joke, like "Let's not start (15) something we can't finish in a cab on Forty-fourth Street"—

TIFFANY: Well, for goodness sake, where was she when you finally did kiss her? On an operating table, under ether?

(20) BOB: No, as it happens she was in a cab on Forty-fourth Street. Somehow or other she got her fingers slammed in the door. She pretended it was nothing, and we were chatting along. (25) Then suddenly—this was blocks later—she started to cry. I looked at her fingers. *(Taking* TIFFANY'S *hand)* Two of the nails were really smashed. And it started out I was just trying to (30) comfort her, and—

TIFFANY: That is the most *un*romantic story I ever heard!

Jean Kerr, *Mary, Mary.*

18. Which of the following best describes the relationship between Bob and Tiffany?

    (1) casual acquaintances
    (2) close friends
    (3) an engaged couple
    (4) brother and sister
    (5) cousins

19. Which of the following best describes Tiffany in this scene?

    (1) supportive
    (2) uninterested
    (3) bored
    (4) worried
    (5) jealous

20. What actually makes Mary's "joke" (line 14) funny?

    (1) She has a way with words.
    (2) Tiffany's answer makes it funny.
    (3) Cab jokes are always funny.
    (4) The couple really did kiss in a cab.
    (5) Pain is often lessened by humor.

21. If Bob ever doesn't want to do something that Tiffany does want to do, how will she probably react?

    (1) by discussing the situation calmly
    (2) by finding another friend to accompany her
    (3) by giving Bob the cold shoulder
    (4) by changing the subject
    (5) by arguing until she gets her way

22. Where did Bob kiss Tiffany?

    (1) in a taxi cab
    (2) in a closet
    (3) on Forty-fourth Street
    (4) in an elevator
    (5) on an operating table

23. Bob finally kissed Mary right after

    (1) she put on her coat
    (2) they got in a cab
    (3) she started to cry
    (4) her fingers were slammed in the door
    (5) he saw her smashed fingernails

Answers begin on page 87.

Unit 1: Popular Literature

Unit 2 Classical Literature
Fiction

Directions: Choose the best answer to each item.

Items 1 and 2 refer to the following excerpt from a novel.

WHO IS THE ENEMY?

" ...look there, friend Sancho Panza, where thirty or more monstrous giants present themselves, all of whom I mean to engage in battle and slay...."
(5) "What giants?" said Sancho Panza.
"Those...with the long arms, and some have them well-nigh two leagues long."
"Look, your worship," said Sancho; "what we see there are not giants but windmills,
(10) and what seem to be their arms are the sails that turned by the wind make the millstone go."
"It is easy to see," replied Don Quixote, "that thou art not used to this business
(15) of adventures; those are giants; and if thou art afraid, away with thee out of this...while I engage them in fierce and unequal combat."

Miguel de Cervantes, *Don Quixote.*

1. Which of the following can you infer from this excerpt?

    (1) Don Quixote has a vivid imagination.
    (2) Don Quixote and Sancho Panza agree on what they are looking at.
    (3) Sancho Panza is a coward.
    (4) Don Quixote and Sancho Panza are not looking at the same objects.
    (5) Don Quixote is afraid of the "giants."

2. Which of the following best describes how Don Quixote would probably react to being greatly outnumbered by enemies in a battle?

    (1) He would be afraid of them.
    (2) He would rely on Sancho Panza to explain things to him.
    (3) He would be unconcerned.
    (4) He would decide to retreat.
    (5) He would attack if Sancho Panza were with him.

Items 3 and 4 refer to the following excerpt from a novel.

WHY IS SCROOGE SATISFIED?

Sitting room, bed-room, lumber-room. All as they should be. Nobody under the table, nobody under the sofa; a small fire in the grate; spoon and basin ready; and
(5) the little saucepan of gruel (Scrooge had a cold in his head) upon the hob. Nobody under the bed; nobody in the closet; nobody in his dressing gown, which was hanging up in a suspicious attitude against
(10) the wall. Lumber-room as usual. Old fire-guard, old shoes, two fish baskets, washing-stand on three legs, and a poker.
Quite satisfied, he closed his door, and locked himself in; double-locked himself in,
(15) which was not his custom. Thus secured against surprise, he took off his cravat; put on his dressing-gown and slippers, and his night-cap; and sat down before the fire to take his gruel.

Charles Dickens, *A Christmas Carol.*

3. The inventory of rooms and objects suggests that this man is
    (1) worried about finding an intruder in his home
    (2) making his will
    (3) surprised at his own neatness
    (4) unfamiliar with the place he is staying
    (5) expecting an old friend

4. The best title for this passage would be
    (1) Bad Habits
    (2) City Night
    (3) The Fright of His Life
    (4) Double-Checking
    (5) As Usual

32 Unit 2: Classical Literature

See Also Literature text Unit 2
Complete Preparation Unit 6, Classical Literature

Items 5–8 refer to the following excerpt from a novel.

WHY ARE THESE TWO MEN DISAGREEING?

...When the bell rang, George waited at the entrance of the "reception room" until a housemaid came through the hall on her way to answer the summons.

(5) "You needn't mind, Mary," he told her. "I'll see who it is and what they want. Probably it's only a pedlar."

"Thank you, sir, Mister George," said Mary; and returned to the rear of the house.

(10) George went slowly to the front door, and halted, regarding the misty silhouette of the caller upon the ornamental frosted glass. After a minute of waiting, this silhouette changed outline so that an arm could be (15) distinguished—an arm outstretched toward the bell, as if the gentleman outside doubted whether or not it had sounded, and were minded to try again. But before the gesture was completed George (20) abruptly threw open the door, and stepped squarely upon the middle of the threshold.

A slight change shadowed the face of Eugene; his look of happy anticipation gave way to something formal and polite. (25) "How do you do, George," he said. "Mrs. Minafer expects to go driving with me, I believe—if you'll be so kind as to send her word that I'm here."

George made not the slightest movement. (30) "No," he said.

Eugene was incredulous, even when his second glance revealed how hot of eye was the haggard young man before him. "I beg your pardon. I said—"

(35) "I heard you," said George. "You said you had an engagement with my mother, and I told you, No!"

Eugene gave him a steady look, and then he asked quietly: "What is the—the (40) difficulty?"

George kept his own voice quiet enough, but that did not mitigate the vibrant fury of it. "My mother will have no interest in knowing that you came for her today," he said. "Or (45) any other day!"

Eugene continued to look at him with a scrutiny in which began to gleam a profound anger, none the less powerful because it was so quiet. "I am afraid I do (50) not understand you."

"I doubt if I could make it much plainer," George said, raising his voice slightly, "but I'll try. You're not wanted in this house, Mr. Morgan, now or at any other time. Perhaps (55) you'll understand—this!"

And with the last word he closed the door in Eugene's face.

Booth Tarkington, *The Magnificent Ambersons*.

5. Which of the following best describes the purpose of Eugene's visit?

   (1) He came to discuss business with George.
   (2) He came to argue with George.
   (3) He had been invited to dinner.
   (4) He came to see George's mother.
   (5) He came to take Mary to the movies.

6. What best explains why George told the housemaid it was probably only a pedlar at the door?

   (1) He honestly didn't know who was at the door.
   (2) He knew the housemaid didn't have any money for a pedlar.
   (3) He didn't want his mother to know Eugene had come.
   (4) He was trying to be helpful to the housemaid.
   (5) He thought it might be the housemaid's boyfriend, whom he would send away.

7. Based on what Eugene says and does in lines 22–40, what can be inferred about what he expected when he rang the bell?

   (1) He expected George to be rude.
   (2) He expected George's mother to answer the door.
   (3) He didn't think anyone would be home.
   (4) He thought George would answer and invite him in.
   (5) He didn't expect any fuss.

8. Which of the following best describes George and Eugene's language and behavior during their conversation?

   (1) refined
   (2) casual
   (3) indifferent
   (4) friendly
   (5) unconventional

Unit 2: Classical Literature

Items 9–13 refer to the following excerpt from a short story.

WHAT DOES CASS FIND AT HOME?

When Cass Edmonds and Uncle Buck ran back to the house from discovering that Tomey's Turl had run again, they heard Uncle Buddy cursing and bellowing
(5) in the kitchen, then the fox and the dogs came out of the kitchen and crossed the hall into the dog's room and they heard them run through the dog's room into his and Uncle Buck's room, then they saw
(10) them cross the hall again into Uncle Buddy's room and heard them run through Uncle Buddy's room into the kitchen again and this time it sounded like the whole kitchen chimney had come down and
(15) Uncle Buddy bellowing like a steamboat blowing, and this time the fox and the dogs and five or six sticks of firewood all came out of the kitchen together with Uncle Buddy in the middle of them hitting at
(20) everything in sight with another stick. It was a good race.

William Faulkner, "Was."

9. Which of the following statements best describes the situation in this passage?
   (1) Uncle Buddy is having a dog race.
   (2) Uncle Buddy is chasing a fox around the kitchen.
   (3) Uncle Buddy is after the dogs that are chasing a fox around the house.
   (4) The dogs are after Uncle Buddy who is chasing the fox.
   (5) The fox is after the dogs who are chasing Uncle Buddy around the kitchen.

10. What probably happened to make it sound "like the whole kitchen chimney had come down" (lines 13–14)?
    (1) Uncle Buddy had hit it with a stick.
    (2) The noise of the race shook the bricks.
    (3) Uncle Buddy's bellowing echoed in the chimney.
    (4) The chase had led though the woodpile by the chimney.
    (5) The chimney had fallen in on Uncle Buddy.

11. Uncle Buck and Uncle Buddy probably think of the dogs as
    (1) excellent fox hunters
    (2) outdoor pets
    (3) good watchdogs
    (4) undisciplined animals
    (5) part of the family

12. Which of the following techniques does the author use to emphasize the chaos of the scene?
    (1) writing a short sentence at the conclusion
    (2) putting all the action in one long sentence
    (3) describing Uncle Buck's and Cass's reaction
    (4) comparing Uncle Buddy's bellowing to a steamboat whistle
    (5) having the action inside the house

13. To which of the following does the author compare Uncle Buddy's bellowing?
    (1) a roaring fire
    (2) a ship's horn
    (3) a dog's bark
    (4) a fox's howl
    (5) a crashing chimney

Unit 2: Classical Literature

Items 14–19 refer to the following excerpt from a novel.

WHAT IS TODAY'S LESSON?

Nat's face had brightened more and more as he listened, for, small as the list of his learning was, it cheered him immensely to feel that he had anything
(5) to fall back upon. "Yes, I can keep my temper—father's beating taught me that. And I can fiddle, though I don't know where the Bay of Biscay is," he thought, with a sense of comfort impossible to
(10) express. Then he said aloud and so earnestly that Demi heard him:

"I *do* want to learn, and I *will* try. I never went to school, but I couldn't help it, and if the fellows don't laugh at me, I guess I'll
(15) get on first rate—you and the lady are so good to me."

"They shan't laugh at you, if they do, I'll—I'll—tell them not to," cried Demi, quite forgetting where he was.

(20) The class stopped in the middle of 7 times 9, and everyone looked up to see what was going on.

Thinking that a lesson in learning to help one another was better than arithmetic just
(25) then, Mr. Bhaer told them about Nat, making such an interesting story out of it that the goodhearted lads all promised to lend him a hand and felt quite honored to be called upon to impart their stores
(30) of wisdom to the chap who fiddled so capitally. This appeal established the right feeling among them, and Nat had a few hindrances to struggle against, for everyone was glad to give him a "boost"
(35) up the ladder of learning.

Louisa May Alcott, *Little Men*.

14. What was the class doing when Demi overheard Nat talking to himself?

    (1) studying quietly
    (2) taking a test
    (3) listening to Mr. Bhaer tell a story
    (4) having a lesson in learning
    (5) reciting the multiplication tables

15. What does the author mean by "stores of wisdom" (lines 29–30)?

    (1) what the boys have learned in school
    (2) the knowledge of the ages
    (3) wise sayings about shopkeeping
    (4) stories about learning
    (5) the best ways to cheat in school

16. Why does Nat decide he can "get on first rate" (line 15) even though he has never been to school before?

    (1) because the other boys volunteer to help him
    (2) because Demi says he can
    (3) because he realizes he already has been able to learn something
    (4) because he realizes that knowing the location of the Bay of Biscay is not important
    (5) because he feels he is a natural scholar

17. As a teacher, Mr. Bhaer could best be described as

    (1) inflexible
    (2) indifferent
    (3) scholarly
    (4) lazy
    (5) sympathetic

18. Which of the following details might Mr. Bhaer have included in his "lesson in learning"?

    (1) that Nat knew the names of the European capitals
    (2) how well Nat played the fiddle
    (3) how important arithmetic is
    (4) what an honor it was to have a scholar like Nat in the class
    (5) how to find out where the Bay of Biscay is

19. The writing style of this passage would be most effective in a book about

    (1) sports heroes
    (2) manners
    (3) self-assertiveness
    (4) political science
    (5) arithmetic

Unit 2: Classical Literature

Nonfiction

Directions: Choose the best answer to each item.

Items 1–5 refer to the following excerpt from an essay.

WHERE IS THE MOTH GOING?

The same energy which inspired the rocks, the ploughmen, the horses, and even, it seemed, the lean bare-backed downs, sent the moth fluttering from side
(5) to side of his square of the window-pane. One could not help watching him. One was, indeed, conscious of a queer feeling of pity for him. The possibilities of pleasure seemed that morning so enormous and so
(10) various that to have only a moth's part in life, and a day moth's at that, appeared a hard fate, and his zest in enjoying his meagre opportunities to the full, pathetic. He flew vigorously to one corner of his
(15) compartment, and, after waiting there a second, flew across to the other. What remained for him but to fly to a third corner and then to a fourth? That was all he could do, in spite of the size of the downs, the
(20) width of the sky, the far-off smoke of houses, and the romantic voice, now and then, of a steamer out at sea. What he could do he did. Watching him, it seemed as if a fibre, very thin but pure, of the
(25) enormous energy of the world had been thrust into his frail and diminutive body. As often as he crossed the pane, I could fancy that a thread of vital light became visible. He was little or nothing but life.

Virginia Woolf, "The Death of the Moth."

1. What is the most probable source for the energy that sends the moth fluttering?

    (1) nature
    (2) sunlight
    (3) the lure of freedom
    (4) the mating instinct
    (5) ambition

2. Which of the following definitions is most probably what the author had in mind when she said the moth had a diminutive body (line 26)?

    (1) rapidly tiring
    (2) stupid
    (3) tiny
    (4) energetic
    (5) romantic

3. What problem would a person be having in the same situation as the moth?

    (1) problems with navigation
    (2) an inability to see the obstacles in life
    (3) too great a desire for pleasure
    (4) being blinded by the light at the window
    (5) an overload of nervous energy

4. Why does the author conclude this passage with the phrase "little or nothing but life" (line 29)?

    (1) because the moth is little
    (2) because the moth means nothing in the larger scheme of life
    (3) because the moth is going to die
    (4) to show her sympathy for the moth
    (5) to suggest that the moth represents the life-force

5. Which of the following best describes why the author feels pity for the moth?

    (1) It is nervous and afraid.
    (2) It is too insignificant a creature to worry about.
    (3) It is pathetic and deserves pity.
    (4) Nobody cares about a moth.
    (5) It doesn't know how limited its existence is.

Items 6–11 refer to the following excerpt from an essay.

WHAT DOES THIS AUTHOR BELIEVE?

Now, it is very likely that men in big industries do these jobs better than the women did them at home. The fact remains that the home contains much
(5) less of interesting activity than it used to contain. What is more, the home has shrunk to the size of a small flat that—even if we restrict woman's job to the bearing and rearing of families—there
(10) is no room for her to do even that. It is useless to urge the modern woman to have twelve children, like her grandmother. Where is she to put them when she has got them? And what modern man wants
(15) to be bothered with them? It is perfectly idiotic to take away woman's traditional occupations and then complain because she looks for new ones. Every woman is a human being—one cannot repeat that
(20) too often—and a human being must have occupation, if he or she is not to become a nuisance to the world.

I am not complaining that the brewing and baking were taken over by men. If
(25) they can brew and bake as well as women or better, then by all means let them do it. But they cannot have it both ways. If they are going to adopt the very sound principle that the job should be done by the person
(30) who does it best, then that rule must be applied universally. If the women make better office-workers than men, they must have the office work. If any individual woman is able to make a first-class lawyer,
(35) doctor, architect or engineer, then she must be allowed to try her hand at it. Once lay down the rule that the job comes first and you throw that job open to every individual, man or woman, fat or thin, tall or short,
(40) ugly or beautiful, who is able to do that job better than the rest of the world.

Dorothy Sayers, "Are Women Human?"

6. The author believes that a job should be offered first to

    (1) any man
    (2) a married man
    (3) any woman who qualifies
    (4) a good office worker
    (5) the best-qualified person

7. When this article was originally published, the average male reader probably

    (1) agreed with Sayers
    (2) disagreed with Sayers
    (3) believed women should be considered first for most jobs
    (4) felt indifferent toward the article
    (5) thought women were better office workers than men

8. Which of the following is a reason that Sayers believes large families are a problem for the modern woman?

    (1) They interfere with her job.
    (2) Her traditional occupations are gone.
    (3) The modern home is too small.
    (4) Men won't stay home with them.
    (5) Children are a nuisance to the world.

9. The author would be most likely to encourage women today to

    (1) protest against discrimination
    (2) give up the job search
    (3) be better office workers
    (4) get training and education
    (5) learn how to brew and bake

10. The tone of this essay could best be described as

    (1) angry
    (2) bitter
    (3) pleading
    (4) resigned
    (5) reasonable

11. Which of the following would the author most likely encourage?

    (1) support gender-neutral hiring policies
    (2) buy a large house and have more children
    (3) learn to brew and bake
    (4) allow women to keep their traditional occupations
    (5) hire only women office workers

Unit 2: Classical Literature   37

Items 12–17 refer to the following excerpt from a book.

WHAT IS THE WORTH OF KNOWLEDGE?

Genuine scholarship is one of the highest successes which our race can achieve. No one is more triumphant than the man who chooses a worthy subject
(5) and masters all its facts and the leading facts of the subjects neighboring. He can then do what he likes. He can, if his subject is the novel, lecture on it chronologically if he wishes because he
(10) has read all the important novels of the past four centuries, many of the unimportant ones, and has adequate knowledge of any collateral facts that bear upon English fiction. The late Sir Walter
(15) Raleigh (who once held this lectureship) was such a scholar. Raleigh knew so many facts that he was able to proceed to influences, and his monograph on the English novel adopts the treatment by
(20) period which his unworthy successor must avoid. The scholar, like the philosopher, can contemplate the river of time. He contemplates it not as a whole, but he can see the facts, the personalities, floating
(25) past him, and estimate the relations between them, and if his conclusions could be as valuable to us as they are to himself he would long ago have civilized the human race. As you know, he has failed.
(30) True scholarship is incommunicable, true scholars rare.

E. M. Forster, *Aspects of the Novel.*

12. The author believes that proof of scholarship lies in
    (1) getting a Ph.D.
    (2) being able to lecture chronologically
    (3) mastering the facts of a worthy subject
    (4) knowing unimportant facts
    (5) knowing about English fiction

13. Why does the author believe that the scholar has failed?
    (1) Not enough books are being written.
    (2) The scholar has not concluded anything.
    (3) Humans still tend to be uncivilized.
    (4) The scholar can't see things as a whole.
    (5) The facts won't help humanity.

14. Forster refers to Sir Walter Raleigh in order to
    (1) remind the reader of Queen Elizabeth
    (2) explain how he got the lectureship
    (3) contemplate the river of time
    (4) explain the importance of the English novel
    (5) provide a well-known example of a true scholar

15. Which of the following ideas is the author suggesting in the last sentence?
    (1) Most people aren't interested in communication.
    (2) Humanity still has a long way to go to be civilized.
    (3) Some people are too lazy to be scholars.
    (4) Scholarship isn't really understandable.
    (5) Civilization can't produce true scholars.

16. To which of the following does the phrase "his unworthy successor" (line 20) refer?
    (1) any scholar
    (2) a philosopher
    (3) Sir Walter Raleigh
    (4) another lecturer
    (5) the author

17. Which of the following best describes advice the author would give to anyone who wants to be a scholar?
    (1) Learn about as many subjects as you can.
    (2) Focus your learning as narrowly as you can.
    (3) Consider all subjects as part of the river of time.
    (4) Concentrate on one subject and other subjects related to it.
    (5) Study all subjects chronologically.

Poetry

Directions: Choose the best answer to each item.

Items 1–3 refer to the following poem.

WHAT IS THIS GIRL DOING?

The Solitary Reaper

Behold her, single in the field,
Yon solitary Highland Lass!
Reaping and singing by herself;
Stop here, or gently pass!
(5) Alone she cuts and binds the grain,
And sings a melancholy strain;
O listen! For the vale profound
is overflowing with the sound.

No Nightingale did ever chaunt
(10) More welcome notes to weary bands
Of travelers in some shady haunt,
Among Arabian sands;
A voice so thrilling ne'er was heard
In springtime from the Cuckoo-bird,
(15) Breaking the silence of the seas
Among the farthest Hebrides.

Will no one tell me what she sings?
Perhaps the plaintive numbers flow
For old, unhappy, far-off things,
(20) And battles long ago:
Or is it some more humble lay,
Familiar matter of today?
Some natural sorrow, loss, or pain,
That has been, and may be again?

(25) Whate'er the theme, the Maiden sang
As if her song could have no ending;
I saw her singing at her work,
And o'er the sickle bending:
I listened, motionless and still;
(30) And, as I mounted up the hill,
The music in my heart I bore,
Long after it was heard no more.

William Wordsworth, *"The Solitary Reaper."*

1. Which of the following statements is not true of the poem?
   (1) The girl's song is sad.
   (2) The girl sings very quietly.
   (3) The girl is working alone.
   (4) The song might be about events of long ago.
   (5) The song might be about some recent event.

2. Which of the following best describes how the last stanza differs from the first three stanzas?
   (1) The speaker uses contractions.
   (2) The speaker uses rhyming lines.
   (3) The speaker shifts the focus to himself.
   (4) The speaker is no longer concerned with the girl and her song.
   (5) The speaker becomes unhappy about what he has seen.

3. Which of the following best summarizes the feeling expressed by the speaker in the last three lines of the poem?
   (1) He will be haunted by the song until he learns the words.
   (2) The scene was pleasing but not memorable.
   (3) This walk was a pleasant way to spend an afternoon.
   (4) This experience will remain in his memory.
   (5) He will write a song based on the singing he has heard.

Items 4–7 refer to the following excerpt from a poem.

WHAT KIND OF PERSON WAS LUCINDA?

I went to the dances at Chandlerville,
And played snap-out at Winchester.
One time we changed partners,
Driving home in the moonlight of middle June,
(5) And then I found Davis.
We were married and lived together for seventy years.
Enjoying, working, raising the twelve children,
Eight of whom we lost
Ere I had reached the age of sixty.
(10) I spun, I wove, I kept the house, I nursed the sick,
I made the garden, and for holiday
Rambled over the fields where sang the larks,
And by Spoon River gathering many a shell,
And many a flower and medicinal weed—
(15) Shouting to the wooded hills, singing to the green valleys.
At ninety-six I had lived enough, that is all,
And passed to a sweet repose.
What is this I hear of sorrow and weariness,
Anger, discontent and drooping hopes?
(20) Degenerate sons and daughters,
Life is too strong for you—
It takes life to love Life.

Edgar Lee Masters, *Spoon River Anthology.*

4. Which of the following best summarizes Lucinda Matlock's life?

   (1) She lived a long life.
   (2) She worked hard for many years.
   (3) She lived an active, happy life.
   (4) She was disappointed in her children.
   (5) She preferred pleasure to work.

5. What is the best explanation for who the "degenerate sons and daughters" (line 20) are?

   (1) her own children
   (2) other children in the town
   (3) previous generations
   (4) later generations
   (5) her own generation

6. What does "Shouting to the wooded hills, singing to the green valleys" (line 15) suggest about Lucinda?

   (1) She had an inner joy.
   (2) She was frivolous.
   (3) She was always glad to escape work.
   (4) She liked to be loud when she could.
   (5) She was a little odd but happy.

7. Which piece of advice would Lucinda most likely give to women today?

   (1) Do what you have to do.
   (2) Don't count on your children.
   (3) Take it easy and life will work out.
   (4) Have fun while you can.
   (5) Work hard, but enjoy life.

Items 8–11 refer to the following poem.

WILL THIS MAN EVER REST?
Is My Team Ploughing?

"Is my team ploughing,
That I was used to drive
And hear the harness jingle
When I was man alive?"

(5) Aye, the horses trample,
The harness jingles now;
No change though you lie under
The land you used to plough.

"Is football playing
(10) Along the river shore,
With lads to chase the leather,
Now I stand up no more?"

Aye, the ball is flying,
The lads play heart and soul;
(15) The goal stands up, the keeper
Stands up to keep the goal.

"Is my girl happy,
That I thought hard to leave,
And has she tired of weeping
(20) As she lies down at eve?"

Aye, she lies down lightly,
She lies not down to weep:
Your girl is well contented.
Be still, my lad, and sleep.

(25) "Is my friend hearty,
Now I am thin and pine,
And has he found to sleep in
A better bed than mine?"

Yes, lad, I lie easy,
(30) I lie as lads would choose;
I cheer a dead man's sweetheart,
Never ask me whose.

A. E. Housman, "Is My Team Ploughing?"

8. The poet uses quotation marks to
   (1) indicate that a man is talking to himself
   (2) show he is quoting from another work
   (3) suggest that there are two speakers
   (4) suggest the speaker is directly addressing the reader
   (5) separate quotation from description

9. Which of the following is not discussed in this poem?
   (1) the land
   (2) the children
   (3) a sweetheart
   (4) death
   (5) a friend

10. Which of the following best describes the condition of the speaker who is asking questions?
    (1) He is asleep.
    (2) He has left the country.
    (3) He has lost his girlfriend.
    (4) He is happy.
    (5) He is dead.

11. Which of the following best expresses the main idea of this poem?
    (1) Friends can't be trusted with women.
    (2) A woman will quickly forget her man.
    (3) Life, in general, continues even after an individual dies.
    (4) The dead can come back from the grave to haunt the living.
    (5) Our souls will live forever.

Unit 2: Classical Literature

Items 12–17 refer to the following poem.

WHAT IS THE NARRATOR WATCHING?

There's Been a Death in the Opposite House

There's been a death in the
   opposite house
As lately as today.
I know it by the numb look
(5) Such houses have a way.

The neighbors rustle in and out,
The doctor drives away.
A window opens like a pod,
Abrupt, mechanically;

(10) Somebody flings a mattress out,
The children hurry by;
They wonder if it died on that,
I used to when a boy.

The minister goes stiffly in
(15) As if the house were his,
And he owned all the mourners now,
And little boys besides;

And then the milliner, and the man
Of the appalling trade,
(20) To take the measure of the house.
There'll be that dark parade

Of tassels and of coaches soon;
It's easy as a sign,
The intuition of the news
(25) In just a country town.

Emily Dickinson, "There's Been a Death in the Opposite House."

12. Which of the following has the speaker not yet seen?

  (1) the neighbors
  (2) the doctor
  (3) the children
  (4) the minister
  (5) the funeral

13. With which of the following words does the poet emphasize the image of the "numb look" (line 4) of the house?

  (1) rustle
  (2) mechanically
  (3) flings
  (4) appalling
  (5) dark

14. What is being described in all but the first and last stanzas?

  (1) the mourners of the dead person
  (2) the horror of death
  (3) the reactions of the speaker
  (4) the activities of the living
  (5) the emotional distress caused by a death

15. Why does the poet use the phrase "it died on that" (line 12) to explain the children's thoughts?

  (1) because that is what the speaker had thought as a child
  (2) to explain why the mattress was thrown out the window
  (3) to explain why the children hurry
  (4) to suggest that death is mysterious and alien to children
  (5) to make clear where the death took place

16. Which of the following describes who the speaker in the poem is?

  (1) a daughter of the deceased
  (2) a man living across the street
  (3) a young neighbor boy
  (4) a son of the deceased
  (5) a woman living next door

17. "The man of the appalling trade" (lines 18–19) most likely refers to

  (1) the mail carrier
  (2) the gardener
  (3) the minister
  (4) the undertaker
  (5) the doctor

Items 18–24 refer to the following poem.

WHY IS THIS MAN ALONE?
Bereft

Where had I heard this wind before
Change like this to a deeper roar?
What would it take my standing there for,
Holding open a restive door,
(5) Looking downhill to a frothy shore?
Summer was past and day was past.
Somber clouds in the west were massed.
Out in the porch's sagging floor
Leaves got up in a coil and hissed,
(10) Blindly struck at my knee and missed.
Something sinister in the tone
Told me my secret must be known:
Word I was in the house alone
Somehow must have gotten abroad,
(15) Word I was in my life alone,
Word I had no one left but God.

Robert Frost, "Bereft."

18. Which of the following best describes the time of day and the season of this poem?

    (1) a summer evening
    (2) a fall afternoon
    (3) a fall evening
    (4) a spring afternoon
    (5) a winter evening

19. Which of the following is the best meaning for sinister (line 11)?

    (1) threatening
    (2) evil
    (3) depressing
    (4) scary
    (5) uneasy

20. To what effect does the poet say that the leaves "got up in a coil and hissed,/Blindly struck at my knee and missed" (lines 9–10)?

    (1) to describe the wind in line 1
    (2) to suggest a striking snake
    (3) to show how nervous the speaker is
    (4) to suggest that the storm has passed
    (5) to explain why the speaker is holding on to the door

21. Which of the following is the best explanation for the fact that abroad (line 14) and God (line 16) don't quite rhyme?

    (1) It is difficult to find a good rhyme for God.
    (2) The poet didn't think it mattered.
    (3) This helps to signal that the poem is finished.
    (4) It weakens the comfort the last line should provide.
    (5) It emphasizes the rhyme in lines 13 and 15.

22. Which of the following is not one of the details of the setting of the poem?

    (1) dark clouds
    (2) wind
    (3) rain
    (4) leaves
    (5) shore

23. Which of the following best describes the speaker's secret (line 12)?

    (1) He wanted to get away for the weekend.
    (2) He is profoundly alone.
    (3) He has lost his religious faith.
    (4) He has returned home.
    (5) His business has failed.

24. Considering the context of the poem, the word bereft in the title probably means

    (1) deprived of a loved one by death
    (2) failed completely at life
    (3) lost all material possessions
    (4) forgotten everything that matters
    (5) suffered disgrace

Unit 2: Classical Literature 43

Items 25–29 refer to the following poem.

WHAT DO WE FIND IN THE SEA?

maggie and milly and molly and may

maggie and milly and molly and may
went down to the beach (to play one day)

and maggie discovered a shell that sang
so sweetly she couldn't remember her troubles, and

(5) milly befriended a stranded star
whose rays languid fingers were;

and molly was chased by a horrible thing
which raced sideways while blowing bubbles: and

may came home with a smooth round stone
(10) as small as a world and as large as alone.

For whatever we lose (like a you or me)
it's always ourselves we find in the sea.

e. e. cummings, "maggie and milly and molly and may."

25. According to the poem, what did the four girls do at the beach?

    (1) They went fishing.
    (2) They got lost.
    (3) They each found something.
    (4) They decided that they were good playmates.
    (5) They fell in love with the sea.

26. It can be inferred from this poem that

    (1) maggie had no trouble
    (2) milly had trouble making friends
    (3) maggie and may were troubled by their discoveries
    (4) molly was more easily scared than the others
    (5) may had the best time

27. Since this poet does not use capital letters in the normal ways, which of the following best explains why he capitalized For in line 11?

    (1) It begins a complete sentence.
    (2) It emphasizes the break between the story and the poet.
    (3) He wanted to break his own rule of capitalization.
    (4) It indicates that the rhythm of the poem is changing.
    (5) It helps to make the poem more lighthearted.

28. The poet probably uses the similes "as small as a world and as large as alone" (line 10) to

    (1) describe the stone realistically
    (2) make the stone seem heavy
    (3) emphasize how round and smooth the stone is
    (4) suggest the mysterious quality may saw in the stone
    (5) compare the stone to maggie's shell

29. Which of the following best describes the effect of the girls' names all beginning with the letter M?

    (1) It implies that the girls are all alike.
    (2) It helps the reader remember the girls' names.
    (3) It gives popular girls' names.
    (4) It provides a boring quality the poet wants.
    (5) It gives the poem a pleasing repetition of sounds.

Drama

Directions: Choose the best answer to each item.

Items 1–4 are based on the following excerpt from a play.

IS BARBARA IN FAVOR OF THIS MARRIAGE?

STEPHEN: I was certainly rather taken aback when I heard they were engaged. Cusins is a very nice fellow, certainly: nobody would ever guess
(5) that he was born in Australia; but—

LADY BRITOMART: Oh, Adolphus Cusins will make a very good husband. After all, nobody can say a word against Greek: it stamps a man at once as an educated
(10) gentleman. And my family, thank Heaven, is not a pig-headed Tory one. We are Whigs, and believe in liberty. Let snobbish people say what they please: Barbara shall marry, not the man they
(15) like, but the man I like.

STEPHEN: Of course I was thinking only of his income. However, he is not likely to be extravagant.

LADY BRITOMART: Don't be too sure of that,
(20) Stephen. I know your quiet, simple, refined poetic people like Adolphus: quite content with the best of everything! They cost more than your extravagant people, who are always
(25) as mean as they are second rate. No: Barbara will need at least £2000 a year. You see it means two additional households. Besides, my dear, you must marry soon. I don't approve of
(30) the present fashion of philandering bachelors and late marriages; and I am trying to arrange something for you.

STEPHEN: It's very good of you, mother; but perhaps I had better arrange that
(35) for myself.

LADY BRITOMART: Nonsense! You are much too young to begin matchmaking: you would be taken in by some pretty little nobody. Of course I don't mean that you
(40) are not to be consulted: you know that as well as I do. *(Stephen closes his lips and is silent.)* Now, don't sulk, Stephen.

George Bernard Shaw, excerpted from *Major Barbara*.

1. When Lady Britomart says, "Barbara shall marry, not the man they like, but the man I like" (lines 14–15), she
   (1) shows how unsnobbish she is
   (2) demonstrates her concern for Barbara's welfare
   (3) helps Stephen understand why she approves of Cusins
   (4) implies that she alone knows what is best for Barbara
   (5) takes a positive stand for the liberty of women

2. When Stephen replies to his mother's offer to arrange his marriage, he is
   (1) being impolite
   (2) making a joke
   (3) encouraged by the idea
   (4) wary of her interference
   (5) eager to find out more

3. According to this passage, which of the following characteristics does not seem to make Adolphus Cusins a good prospect as a husband?
   (1) He is a very nice fellow.
   (2) He was born in Australia.
   (3) He is an educated man.
   (4) People like Adolphus are content with the best.
   (5) He will not be extravagant.

4. What response did the author of the play probably intend the audience to have to this scene?
   (1) sadness
   (2) anger
   (3) confusion
   (4) sulkiness
   (5) amusement

Items 5–10 refer to the following excerpt from a play.

WILL THE GUESTS ENJOY THE PARTY?

(THE COLONEL's *valet,* BENGTSSON, *wearing livery, enters from the hall, accompanied by* JOHANSSON, *who is dressed very formally as a waiter.*)

(5) BENGTSSON: Now, Johansson, you'll have to wait on the table while I take care of the coats. Have you done this before?

JOHANSSON: During the day I push that war chariot, as you know, but in
(10) the evenings I work as a waiter at receptions. It's always been my dream to get into the house. They're peculiar people, aren't they?

BENGTSSON: Well, yes, I think one might
(15) say that they're a little strange.

JOHANSSON: Are we going to have a musicale this evening? Or what is the occasion?

BENGTSSON: Just the ordinary ghost
(20) supper, as we call it. They drink tea, without saying a word, or else the Colonel talks all by himself. And they champ their biscuits and crackers all at once and all in unison. They sound like
(25) a pack of rats in an attic.

JOHANSSON: Why do you call it the ghost supper?

BENGTSSON: They all look like ghosts. This has been going on for twenty
(30) years—always the same people, always saying the same things. Or else keeping silent to avoid being embarrassed.

August Strindberg, excerpted from *The Ghost Sonata.*

5. This scene is most probably taking place in
   (1) an attic
   (2) a rich man's house
   (3) a haunted house
   (4) the house of Johansson's regular employer
   (5) a restaurant

6. If Bengtsson were a graduate student instead of a valet, which of the following groups would he probably talk about in the same way?
   (1) the older faculty members
   (2) the undergraduates
   (3) the secretarial staff
   (4) his closest friends
   (5) a group of musicians

7. From this exchange, what might the audience expect later in the play?
   (1) a lively musical event
   (2) a gala dinner party
   (3) the appearance of a ghost
   (4) unusual conversation between people
   (5) a happy ending

8. For what major purpose has the author included Johansson in this scene?
   (1) to be an extra waiter
   (2) as comic relief for Bengtsson
   (3) to introduce him as a primary character
   (4) to make Bengtsson look foolish
   (5) to provide further information about the household

9. Which of the following best explains why Johansson doesn't know about the ghost suppers?
   (1) He has worked only on musicale evenings.
   (2) He has never worked in this house before.
   (3) He has been working in this house only during the day.
   (4) He has always thought the people were strange.
   (5) He has only taken care of the coats before.

10. Based on the excerpt, which of the following best describes how well Bengtsson knows Johansson?
    (1) He doesn't know Johansson at all.
    (2) He has just met Johansson this evening.
    (3) He has known Johansson for twenty years.
    (4) He knows Johansson slightly.
    (5) He can't remember if he has ever met Johansson.

Items 11–15 refer to the following excerpt from a play.

WHY IS HELENA'S LIFE DREARY?

HELENA: You hate Alexander without reason; he is like every one else, and no worse than you are.

VOITSKI: If you could only see your face, (5) your gestures. Oh, how tedious your life must be.

HELENA: It is tedious, yes and dreary! You all abuse my husband and look on me with compassion; you think, "Poor (10) woman, she is married to an old man." How well I understand your compassion! As Astroff said just now, see how you thoughtlessly destroy the forests, so that there will be none left. So you also (15) destroy mankind, and soon fidelity and purity and self-sacrifice will have vanished with the woods. Why cannot you look calmly at a woman unless she is yours? Because, the doctor was (20) right, you are possessed by a devil of destruction; you have no mercy on the woods or the birds or on women or on one another.

VOITSKI: I don't like your philosophy.

(25) HELENA: That doctor has a sensitive, weary face—an interesting face. Sonia evidently likes him, and she is in love with him, and I can understand it. This is the third time he has been here since (30) I have come, and I have not had a real talk with him yet or made much of him. He thinks I am disagreeable. Do you know Ivan, the reason you and I are such friends? I think it is because we (35) are both lonely and unfortunate. Don't look at me in that way, I don't like it.

VOITSKI: How can I look otherwise when I love you? You are my joy, my life, and my youth. I know that my chances (40) of being loved in return are infinitely small, do not exist, but I ask nothing of you. Only let me look at you, listen to your voice—

HELENA: Hush, someone will overhear you.
(45) *(They go toward the house.)*

VOITSKI: *(following her)* Let me speak to you my love, do not drive me away, and this alone will be my greatest happiness!

(50) HELENA: Ah! This is agony!

Anton Chekhov, *Uncle Vanya*.

11. If Helena were asked to write an essay, she would probably
    (1) write clearly and concisely
    (2) be too timid to accept the assignment
    (3) write about everything except the assigned topic
    (4) use a humorous tone
    (5) write in a scientific manner

12. Which of the following would be the best title for this passage?
    (1) The Doctor's Advice
    (2) Man and his Environment
    (3) In Defense of Her Husband
    (4) The Ignored Suitor
    (5) Helena's Hope

13. How does the author intend Voitski to appear in this scene?
    (1) as a jolly kidder
    (2) as a melodramatic person
    (3) as a patient and sincere lover
    (4) as rude and insensitive
    (5) as a gentle and understanding friend

14. To what is Voitski referring when he says "I don't like your philosophy" (line 24)?
    (1) Helena's reliance on Astroff's opinion
    (2) that Helena objects to the destruction of forests
    (3) that Helena believes the doctor is right
    (4) Helena's statement that men have no mercy
    (5) Helena's objection to the compassion of men

15. Which of the following characters are described as friends because they are both unfortunate?
    (1) Helena and Voitski
    (2) Sonia and Voitski
    (3) Helena and Alexander
    (4) Sonia and Helena
    (5) Voitski and Alexander

Answers begin on page 93.

Unit 3 Commentary

Literature

Directions: Choose the best answer to each item.

Items 1–4 refer to the following excerpt from a book review.

HOW DOES A WRITER DEAL WITH GRIEF?

Isabel Allende, the distinguished Chilean writer, was celebrating the publication of one of her novels at a Barcelona party in December 1991, when she got word that
(5) her daughter was in a hospital in Madrid. She flew to her side. "I love you too, Mama," the 27-year-old Paula murmured just before she was seized by convulsions and fell into a coma. She never woke up, and a
(10) year later she died in Allende's arms. "I had a choice," the author recalls. "Was I going to commit suicide? Sue the hospital? Or was I going to write a book that would heal me?"
(15) *Paula* (Harper Collins; 330 pages; $24) the memoir Allende began on yellow pads as she sat in the hospital, is written as an anguished letter to her daughter, who suffered from porphyria—a metabolic
(20) disorder that is rarely fatal. "They told me she would wake up in a week or two," the writer says. But months passed at Paula's bedside before Allende learned that a hospital mishap had caused irreversible
(25) brain damage. "It was destiny—and it was bad luck. After they told me, I went on writing because I could not stop. I could not let anger destroy me."
The book, as much a celebration of
(30) Allende's turbulent life as the chronicle of Paula's death, is a best seller in the U.S., Latin America and Europe. It has brought a new audience to the author, 52, who wrote her first novel, *The House of*
(35) *the Spirits*, at 40, when she was an exile in Venezuela after the murder of her cousin, former Chilean President Salvador Allende. That novel, in the magical realist style of Gabriel Garcia Marquez, was made into a
(40) 1994 film with Meryl Streep and Jeremy Irons. Altogether, Allende's four novels and a short-story collection have sold an estimated 10 million copies worldwide. *Paula* is her first nonfiction work—a book,
(45) she says, "I have been rehearsing all my life to write."

Margot Hornblower, "Grief and Rebirth," *Time*.

1. Which of the following statements best describes what Isabel Allende has written?

    (1) She has written only novels.
    (2) Everything she has written is a true experience.
    (3) She has never written short stories.
    (4) She has written both fiction and nonfiction.
    (5) She has written a screenplay about Salvador Allende.

2. According to the review, Isabel Allende wrote *Paula*

    (1) so that she could sue the hospital
    (2) as a way of coping with her grief
    (3) in order to explain what destiny is
    (4) so that it could later become a movie
    (5) to explain the symptoms of porphyria

3. If Isabel Allende herself were to become gravely ill, she would most likely

    (1) blame her doctors
    (2) commit suicide
    (3) consider it her fate
    (4) never write again
    (5) turn the experience into a poem

See Also | Literature and the Arts | Unit 3
Complete Preparation | Unit 6, Commentary

4. Which of the following inferences about the author of the review can be made from this excerpt?

   (1) The author has a high opinion of Allende's work.
   (2) The author thinks all of Allende's books should be made into movies.
   (3) The author thinks Allende's own life is too much a part of this book.
   (4) The author thinks Allende overreacted to the death of her daughter.
   (5) The author thinks Allende should have started writing at an earlier age.

Items 5–8 refer to the following book review.

SO WHAT IS WRONG WITH HISTORY?

Any list of trivia yields up some general truths, and the insightful reader will glean much from *Legends, Lies, and Cherished Myths of American History*. Richard
(5) Shenkman, a co-author of *One Night Stands With American History*, has cobbled together 17 brief chapters to set us straight on such topics as discoverers and inventors, the good old days, education,
(10) art and other subjects both serious and light. We learn that sleeping cars were around long before George Pullman, that in the 1920's and 1930's high school drop out rates were higher than today; that
(15) Emanuel Leutze, in his painting *Washington Crossing the Delaware*, may have been trying not to rouse American patriots but to stir up revolution in his native Germany. The author relies mainly on other people's
(20) research, which does not keep him from making some statements that go clunk in the night, for example his claim that "Warren Harding...may have been the victim of more myths than any other
(25) [President]." His chapter on slavery, on the other hand, is very good. He shows that most of the standard histories— written by Northern whites—undervalue the extent of Southern whites' opposition
(30) to slavery and vastly overstate the role of the Underground Railroad. Facts go only skin-deep, but they can prickle memorably, which is why books like this, disabusing us of our cherished bunk, are useful and fun.

James Cornelius, Review of *Legends, Lies, and Cherished Myths of American History*, by Richard Shenkman.

5. What is the reviewer's opinion of Shenkman's book?

   (1) It isn't as entertaining as his last book was.
   (2) He believes the trivia is boring.
   (3) He thinks that the topics are poorly chosen.
   (4) He believes it abuses historical facts.
   (5) It is generally entertaining and informative.

6. Which of the following is not suggested in this review?

   (1) that George Pullman is associated with sleeping cars
   (2) that people are concerned about modern drop out rates
   (3) that Shenkman has done his own thorough research
   (4) that other American histories may be misleading
   (5) that people may believe things that are not based on fact

7. The reviewer helps the reader understand the phrase "that go clunk in the night" (lines 21–22) means unsuccessful by

   (1) referring to other people's research
   (2) explaining it in detail
   (3) using the example of Emanuel Leutze
   (4) saying "on the other hand, is very good" (lines 25–26)
   (5) claiming that "facts only go skin-deep" (lines 31–32)

8. Which of the following best defines what the reviewer means by bunk (line 34)?

   (1) general truths
   (2) a type of bed
   (3) statement of facts
   (4) historical events
   (5) legends and myths

Items 9–12 refer to the following book review.

WHAT HAPPENED TO THE SOLDIERS?

There is a truth to war. It lies beyond the offices of political leaders, where lofty principle provides the reason and the rationalization; out past the war rooms
(5) where grand strategies calmly, even detachedly, take shape; even away from the tents of the generals, where glory and devotion to duty are often the watchwords.

It's in the mud and the blood, and in the
(10) minds of men. It says that cruelty begets cruelty, reaction overpowers reason, and the enemy is likely to rise up not so much from the next trench as from the depths of a man's soul. And it is a truth that is apparent
(15) throughout *Prisoners of Twilight*, Don Robertson's riveting novel of the Civil War.

It is April of 1865. The war is nearly over and a ragtag group of Southern soldiers near the falling Confederate capital of
(20) Richmond has been forced into the battle of their lives—not with the Union forces, but with hunger, exhaustion, and the realization that their cause has failed. Their main objective has become merely
(25) to stay alive while trying to get home.

Most are simple men, still wanting to be led when there are no leaders, men who have tried to overcome the hurdles of their lives with physical reactions rather than
(30) reasoned response. Now, when reason is needed to lift them from the depths, to save them from themselves, they are incapable of it.

Complicating matters is the presence in
(35) the same Virginia countryside of another small band of Southerners led by a general for whom the war will never end. Orders are orders, rules are rules; and surrender is unthinkable. That his devotion to duty
(40) amid the shambles of war has driven him insane is not enough of a reason for his still well-drilled band to stop following him and obeying his irrational demands.

By shaping each chapter from
(45) the viewpoint of a different participant, Robertson slips into the lives of the men of each group. His flashbacks help the reader understand why each man acts the way he
(50) does, even when the man himself doesn't.

David E. Jones, "Human Sacrifices to the God of War."

9. According to this article, Robertson explores the Civil War
   (1) in order to discover why the Confederacy lost
   (2) through the experiences of individual soldiers
   (3) as a critical study of military discipline
   (4) to explain the consequences of battle fatigue
   (5) from the point of view of a Southern general

10. What is suggested in this review about the "truth to war" (line 1)?
    (1) War is the conflict between grand strategies and failed causes.
    (2) Calm reasoning is the key to victory.
    (3) Strict devotion to duty leads to insanity.
    (4) War is a game played by politicians who use simple men as their battle pieces.
    (5) The reality of war involves raw emotion, not logic.

11. Why is the sentence "It's in the mud and blood, and in the minds of men" (lines 9–10) an effective beginning for the second paragraph?
    (1) It creates a powerful basic image of the battlefield.
    (2) It explains how cruelty develops.
    (3) The title of the book is based on these images.
    (4) It reminds the reader of why men go to war.
    (5) It echoes the concepts of glory and duty.

12. Why does the reviewer use the phrase "for whom the war will never end" (line 37)?
    (1) to illustrate how exhausted the men are
    (2) because the general had not heard that the war is almost over
    (3) to suggest that the general wants to keep fighting for his cause
    (4) to suggest the extent of the general's insanity
    (5) as an example of the workings of a military mind

Items 13–17 refer to the following book review.

WHAT HAPPENED IN COOK COUNTY?

When we first meet the Honorable Raymond Sodini, his industrial-strength hangover has prompted him to call his office: "I was out late last night. Tell Cy to
(5) put on the robes and do the bum call." And once again, Police Sgt. Cy Martin has donned his judicial disguise to face the morning's smelly clutch of vagrants plucked from Chicago's streets. Sodini's
(10) frequent relegation of his judgeship to a cop constituted more than malfeasance. It also invited pranks. Take one day, for example, a particularly bellicose drunk irked Martin. Martin eventually released
(15) him—but not before startling the drunk with his "sentence": death.

For decades the real butt of these shenanigans were the citizens of Cook County, Ill. In the early 1980's an ambitious
(20) federal sting, Operation Greylord, explored the nation's largest local court system and found it to be a nest of corruption. Five years of subsequent trials yielded more than 80 convictions of judges, attorneys,
(25) court clerks, sheriff's deputies and police officers. In *Greylord*, a gritty romp past hustlers, bagmen, and scoundrels, authors James Tuohy and Rob Warden use evidence from the trials to describe a
(30) bribe-happy gang of legal weasels whose motto might have been the immortal words of Judge Wayne W. Olson: "I love people that take dough because you know exactly where you stand."

(35) Among the most avaricious justices described in the book was John J. (Dollars) Devine. He sold courtroom favors to lawyers for $200 but once gave a $50 discount to a newcomer who, it turned out,
(40) was a government mole. Prices were lower in traffic court, where a group of lawyers known as "miracle workers" routinely paid Judge Richard LeFevour $100 to fix drunk-driving cases. The
(45) judge's bagman was his cousin, a policeman named Jimmy LeFevour, who collected dues with a not-so-gentle reminder: "I'm here. Fill me up." At times it was difficult to maintain the charade
(50) of justice. One judge managed to acquit a miracle worker's client despite her testimony that she was indeed drunk while driving, saying: "I still have reasonable doubt."

John McCormick, "Fun and Games in the Windy City."

13. The first paragraph is best summarized by which of the following sentences?

    (1) The judge sentenced a drunk to death.
    (2) A policeman frequently took the place of a judge who had a hangover.
    (3) Chicago police are prone to playing pranks.
    (4) Raymond Sodini had a sense of humor.
    (5) Chicago's streets are filled with smelly bums.

14. A common crime included in the "nest of corruption" (line 22) in the Cook County court system was

    (1) bootlegging
    (2) hustling
    (3) impersonation of a police officer
    (4) tampering with evidence
    (5) bribery

15. With which of the following quotations would John J. Devine have been least likely to agree?

    (1) Time is money.
    (2) Make hay while the sun shines.
    (3) Waste not, want not.
    (4) Honesty is the best policy.
    (5) Familiarity breeds contempt.

16. A person accused of drunk driving under today's laws would probably wish there were still access to

    (1) Police Sgt. Cy Martin
    (2) a judge's bagman
    (3) a miracle worker
    (4) Operation Greylord
    (5) Raymond Sodini

17. From the information in the excerpt, which of the following inferences can you make about Cook County in the 1980s?

    (1) Justice could be bought.
    (2) Only the rich went to jail.
    (3) Money was not an important factor.
    (4) Judges all had integrity.
    (5) The justice system worked well.

Unit 3: Commentary   51

TV and Film

Directions: Choose the best answer to each item.

Items 1–4 are based on the following excerpt from a movie review.

WAS THIS A GOOD PERFORMANCE?

In the middle of *My Left Foot*, the movie about the Dubliner Christy Brown, a victim of cerebral palsy who became a painter and writer, Christy (Daniel Day-Lewis) is in
(5) a restaurant, at a dinner party celebrating the opening of an exhibition of the pictures he painted by holding a brush between his toes. For some time, he has been misinterpreting the friendly manner of the
(10) woman doctor who has been training him, and who arranged the show, and now, high on booze and success, he erupts. "I love you, Eileen," he says, and then, sharing his happiness with the others
(15) at the table, "I love you all." Eileen, not comprehending that his love for her is passionate and sexual, takes the occasion to announce that she's going to marry the gallery owner in six months. In his
(20) staccato, distorted speech, Christy spits out "Con-grat-u-la-tions" so that the syllables sound like slaps, and then he lashes her with "I'm glad you taught me to speak so I could say that, Eileen." The
(25) restaurant is suddenly quiet: everyone is watching his torment as he beats his head on the table and yanks the tablecloth off with his teeth.

It's all very fast, and it may be the most
(30) emotionally wrenching scene I've ever experienced at the movies. The greatness of Day-Lewis's performance is that he pulls you inside Christy Brown's frustration and rage (and his bottomless thirst).
(35) There's nothing soft or maudlin about this movie's view of Christy. Right from the first shot, it's clear that the Irish playwright-director Jim Sheridan, who wrote the superb screenplay with another Irish
(40) playwright, Shane Connaughton, knows what he's doing. Christy's left foot is starting a record on his turntable; there's a scratchy stop, and the foot starts it up again—Mozart's *Cosi Fan Tutte*. A few
(45) toes wriggle to the music, and then in a sudden cut the bearded head of the man that the musical toes belong to jerks into the frame, and we see the tight pursed mouth, the tense face, and the twisted-
(50) upward, lolling head with slitted eyes peering down. He's anguished and locked in yet excitingly insolent. Day-Lewis seizes the viewer; he takes possession of you. His interpretation recalls Olivier's
(55) crookbacked, long-nosed Richard III; Day-Lewis's Christy Brown has the sexual seductiveness that was so startling in the Olivier Richard.

Pauline Kael, review of *My Left Foot*.

1. How would the reviewer rate Day-Lewis's performance?
   (1) poor
   (2) mediocre
   (3) fair
   (4) better than average
   (5) superb

2. Which of the following best summarizes the reviewer's opinion of the director of the movie?
   (1) The reviewer thinks the director could have gotten better sound quality in the movie.
   (2) The reviewer thinks the director is too soft with Christy.
   (3) The reviewer is glad the director is Irish.
   (4) The reviewer is impressed with the director's skill.
   (5) The reviewer isn't sure the director is good until the end of the film.

3. When the reviewer writes, "Day-Lewis seizes the viewer; he takes possession of you" (lines 52–53), she means the actor's performance is
   (1) frightening
   (2) out of control
   (3) powerful
   (4) disgusting
   (5) disrespectful

4. As it is used in this excerpt, the best meaning for staccato (line 20) is
   (1) loud
   (2) disconnected
   (3) garbled
   (4) angry
   (5) unfamiliar

Items 5–8 are based on the following TV review.

WHO IS GOING TO LIKE THESE SHOWS?

(5) Creature features—meaning films starring cuddly, lovable critters, not menacing monsters—often sink or swim on the natural animal magnetism of the lead. And the title character of 1994's "Andre" has verve and charisma to spare. The "bad-smelling, fish-eating, raspberry-blowing" seal adopted by a Maine clan dances, claps, mugs, paints, sleds and
(10) even manages to work a TV. This fact-based heartwarmer (airing Saturday at 8 P.M. [ET] on HBO) stays afloat thanks to its flippery star's buoyant charms. The slapstick antics of Andre and his best
(15) friend Toni (played by the endearingly wistful Tina Majorino), coupled with some nail-biting life-or-death action sequences and eye-catching underwater photography, make this fare fit for the entire family.
(20) After emerging from the sea, head deep into the woods Sunday when CBS presents "Call of the Wild." Based loosely on Jack London's classic, the 1993 TV movie repeat follows a determined
(25) prospector (the convincing Rick Schroder) and his brave canine companion Buck in the Yukon of the 1890's.
Farley Drexel Hatcher a.k.a. Fudge is a bit of a wild child whose misadventures
(30) are chronicled Saturdays on ABC. The network sneaks in the second-season premiere this week with an A-plus outing about a take-home aptitude test that Fudge's brother Peter must complete.
(35) When Peter unknowingly returns a test copy that Fudge filled out, his sibling's scores weigh in at genius level and leave Peter with the embarrassment of "having a brother half [his] age but twice as smart."
(40) Luke Tarsitano is a rambunctious delight in the title role.
A less precocious though supremely talented bunch of kids assemble Thursday on the Disney Channel for the fourth annual
(45) Disney's Young Musicians Symphony Orchestra concert. The performance is the culmination of a 10-day camp that brought 75 musically gifted youngsters (age 12 and under) together with renowned composers,
(50) conductors and instructors. Highlights include a solo by Judy Kuhn (the singing voice of "Pocahontas"), who does a beautiful rendition of the film's "Colors of the Wind," as well as appearances by
(55) classical guitarist Christopher Parkening and the Pacific Chorale Children's Chorus. CBS *This Morning's* Paula Zahn hosts.

Ray Stackhouse, "The adventures of 'Andre'—a seal with splashy appeal," *TV Guide*.

5. Which of the following phrases best summarizes this review?

   (1) an unrelated assortment of programs
   (2) programs for the new TV season
   (3) a guide to good children's programs
   (4) TV shows for animal lovers
   (5) a group of award-winning programs

6. According to the review, which of the following is not a factor in making "Andre" successful?

   (1) the underwater photography
   (2) an engaging animal actor
   (3) the actress who plays Toni
   (4) a serious story
   (5) exciting action

7. Based on the review, which of the following inferences can be made about the program "Fudge"?

   (1) It is a weekly show.
   (2) It features an animal character.
   (3) It is about a young musician.
   (4) Fudge is a poor student.
   (5) Only repeat episodes of the show are available.

8. Which of the following types of programs are not included in this review?

   (1) outdoor adventure
   (2) science fiction
   (3) musical performance
   (4) comedy
   (5) classic literature

Items 9–12 are based on the following TV review.

WHAT MAKES A TV SHOW FUNNY?

The other night, I laughed at a *Murphy Brown* rerun—and I realized it was the first time *Murphy* had made me laugh in I don't know how long. Yet I still hadn't given up
(5) on the show. I kept watching out of loyalty, or perhaps optimism, or just inertia, that intense gravity created by my couch. For TV is a powerful habit, strong enough to keep me watching a show even after its
(10) quality has declined.

I don't know precisely when *Murphy* lost its pow. When it premiered in 1988, I became a fervent fan. *Murphy* had attitude about politics, business, and TV itself. And
(15) thanks to good-hearted Eldin the painter (Robert Pastorelli), it also had enough serendipity to round its sharp edges. It had an ensemble that fit like a jigsaw puzzle. It had timing. It had laughs.

(20) But sometime since, *Murphy* lost its touch. The first half of most episodes is still OK, but that only sets up what is inevitably a disappointing second half. The show tries too hard. It falls flat. I don't
(25) know why. Maybe it's simply because *Murphy's* creator, Diane English, left to make *Love & War* (oops). Or maybe it was the departure of Eldin or the arrival of McGovern (no, the show slumped before
(30) he left and she came). Or maybe it was the series of plot detours that broke the spell and made me suspend my suspended disbelief (if it can happen to a drama—if *Dallas* can be ruined by a
(35) shower scene—then it can happen to a sitcom). There have been many wrong turns: Murphy (Candice Bergen) has had more dead-end romances than *Cheers'* Sam Malone. And her maternity has not
(40) been entirely credible; in some episodes, her son might as well be a lamp. But at least her pregnancy did produce an entertaining national debate. And speaking of Dan Quayle, maybe that's the
(45) cause of *Murphy's* fall: She doesn't have him to kick around anymore.

I still can't finger the culprit. I do know *Murphy* has tried hard not to stagnate but to let its cast grow and occasionally
(50) surprise. After Corky (Faith Ford) married and divorced, she finally emerged as a real person with a brain and a soul. Miles (Grant Shaud) has managed to face Maalox choices that alternately define him
(55) as a good guy or a spineless corporate toady. Jim (Charles Kimbrough) has become more than just a deep voice. Even Frank (Joe Regalbuto) has tried hard—though he still grates. Yet at the end of
(60) most *Murphys*, I'm left deflated. Maybe there are only so many temp-secretary jokes a show can make. Or maybe there are only so many years a brilliant show can stay brilliant.

Jeff Jarvis, "The Couch Critic," *TV Guide*.

9. Which of these characters does the author of the review like the least?

(1) Eldin
(2) Corky
(3) Miles
(4) Murphy
(5) Frank

10. The author implies that as a character in the show, Murphy's son

(1) is important
(2) is insignificant
(3) is entertaining
(4) adds needed humor
(5) interferes with the humor

11. Which statement best expresses the reviewer's overall opinion of the show?

(1) The characters aren't interesting.
(2) Some episodes are very good and others are terrible.
(3) Episodes are predictable and boring.
(4) The show's creative staff is not as good as it once was.
(5) Most episodes have weak endings.

12. If you were to read a review this author wrote when *Murphy Brown* premiered, which of the following opinions would you probably find?

(1) This show might be worth watching.
(2) This show probably won't make it.
(3) This is an outstanding show.
(4) This is just another comedy show.
(5) This show is good, but nothing special.

Items 13–16 refer to the following excerpt from a movie review.

WHAT IS RAYMOND'S SPECIAL TALENT?

Raymond Babbitt (Dustin Hoffman) is an autistic savant. He has lived most of his life in an institution, for the world outside poses too many dangers. Incapable of
(5) emotional connections to other people, he retreats into a world of rituals and compulsions. If the furniture in his room is misplaced, if he doesn't get to watch *The People's Court* at the appointed time, or if
(10) someone touches him, he bleats like a frightened goat and throws a tantrum. But he has a gift: ask him to multiply 312 by 183 and he'll instantly know the answer. Drop a box of toothpicks on the floor and
(15) he'll tell you exactly how many toothpicks have fallen. He's like a computer, but not one you'd call user-friendly.

Imagine crossing the country in an old convertible with such a man. That's what
(20) Charlie Babbitt (Tom Cruise), Raymond's younger brother, must do. And that, in a sense is the "plot" of *Rain Main*, director Barry Levinson's fascinating, touching and unsettling character study. It's not really
(25) about Raymond, however, who can't change. It's about Charlie, who never knew he had a brother until his despised father dies and leaves a $3 million trust fund to Raymond, cutting Charlie out of
(30) the family fortune. Charlie, an angry young hustler who sells imported cars in L.A., virtually kidnaps his brother from his institution in Cincinnati and drives off in the family '49 Buick Roadmaster with his
(35) Italian girlfriend (Valerie Golino) and Raymond, hoping to squeeze half the inheritance out of the doctor who controls the trust.

It's not hard to guess that the insensitive,
(40) money-grubbing hotshot will undergo a transformation of the heart by the time this cross-country odyssey wends its way to the West Coast. And given Hollywood's history of treating dysfunctional characters as
(45) sentimental saints, one had reason to fear the worst. But *Rain Main*, written by Ronald Bass and Barry Morrow, is full of smart surprises. One of its considerable pleasures is watching Levinson and his cast deftly
(50) avoid every major pothole in sight.

Bracingly unsentimental—but not unmoving—and funny in a way that never exploits Raymond's disorder. *Rain Main* is a movie about a man learning to take the first
(55) steps toward love, even when there is no realistic hope that love can be returned.

David Ansen, "Taking the High Road."

13. Which of the following is the best definition for <u>odyssey</u> (line 42)?
   (1) a change of heart
   (2) a complicated chase
   (3) a character study
   (4) a journey in search of something
   (5) a sentimental trip

14. According to this review, the focus in *Rain Man* is on
   (1) Charlie Babbitt learning to love
   (2) Charlie Babbitt stealing his brother's inheritance
   (3) Raymond Babbitt overcoming his autism
   (4) Raymond Babbitt learning to love his brother
   (5) Raymond Babbitt learning to use his gift

15. What the reviewer calls "Hollywood's history of treating dysfunctional characters as sentimental saints" (lines 43-45) is most similar to the way movies often have
   (1) portrayed families as loving
   (2) glorified outlaws
   (3) pictured cowboys as tough
   (4) sentimental love scenes
   (5) shown gangsters to be unpleasant characters

16. Raymond is compared to a non-user-friendly computer in order to illustrate
   (1) how well he will fit into the business world
   (2) how far he has retreated into his own world
   (3) his amazing mathematical ability
   (4) the growing use of technology in movies
   (5) the reviewer's familiarity with computers

Visual Arts

Directions: Choose the best answer to each item.

Items 1–4 refer to the following review.

WHY ARE THEY ALL BUYING WEDGWOOD?

For most people, the name Wedgwood immediately brings to mind mass-produced blue-and-white ware. But, for contemporary potters, the most significant aspect of
(5) Wedgwood production (from the 18th century on) is marketing. Josiah Wedgwood and his heirs should be credited with making Wedgwood a household word.

First among Josiah's clever marketing
(10) moves was plainly marking the ware on the bottom. And if a product line was imitated, he would order the colors and shapes changed to stay a step ahead of the competition. Yet the key to success
(15) was publicity. Wedgwood was among the first to publish illustrated catalogs.

Today, the Wedgwood Group rarely passes up an opportunity for publicity. Press packets, announcing the production
(20) of new lines, commemorative and limited-edition items are issued frequently.

However, the latest in marketing involves educating not just the public, but retailers as well. At the annual exhibition
(25) of new products in Barlaston, England, last February, the tableware designs were classified in three groups—classic, country and fine white— "which reflect modes in home furnishing and decor,
(30) and which have been devised to help customers make their choice of china design." Then the work was displayed in room settings, designed by Wedgwood, to present these three collections in
(35) appropriate environments.

Buyers were also informed of "exciting sales support and advertising programs planned for the year," and had the opportunity to preview a video designed
(40) to assist the retailer by providing basic training for sales personnel.

In the past, larger-volume studio potters, and the more-commercial hand producers have followed trends from industry. Perhaps
(45) direct sales assistance and marketing to retailers will follow in studio ceramics.

Ceramics Monthly, "Wedgwood Then and Now."

1. In the reviewer's opinion, the February exhibition was important as an example of Wedgwood's
   (1) press packets about new production lines
   (2) education of the public
   (3) publicity and marketing techniques
   (4) staying ahead of the competition
   (5) illustrated catalogs

2. If Josiah Wedgwood were a modern businessman, he would probably do all but which of the following?
   (1) have a highly trained research staff
   (2) advertise on television
   (3) add new designs to his traditional china patterns
   (4) present a set of china to the Queen of England
   (5) refuse to use computer technology

3. Which of the following is a result of the imitation of Wedgwood's product lines?
   (1) a lot of poor-quality china
   (2) a variety of Wedgwood designs for modern customers
   (3) a growth in the number of studio potters
   (4) the practice of marking the bottom of the ware
   (5) production of limited-edition items

4. If studio potters continue to follow industry trends, they will probably
   (1) imitate Wedgwood designs
   (2) develop larger markets for their work
   (3) join the Wedgwood Group
   (4) limit the number of designs they use
   (5) lose sales to Wedgwood

Items 5–8 refers to the following review.

WHAT DISTINGUISHED THIS PAINTER'S WORK?

Peter Paul Rubens, Raphael and others produced magnificent paintings of biblical events showing saints, cherubs, and surprisingly, distinguished contemporaries.
(5) It was not uncommon to include among the crowd or even as principal worshipers patrons and the court in their very best finery, even a suit of armour.

The settings, too, might be the cathedral
(10) in town or a Lombardy landscape with shepherds joined by Crusaders and ruling dukes.

How Rubens included contemporary portraits in his biblical and allegorical
(15) paintings was illustrated by Christopher J. White, who lectured in Muncie earlier this month.

The distinguished art historian, director of the Ashmolean Museum at Oxford
(20) University, delivered the second annual Edmund F. Petty Memorial Lecture at the Ball State University Art Gallery.

Author of several books, including *Peter Paul Rubens: Man and Artist*,
(25) White's topic focused on Rubens and the Art of Portraiture.

"Although Rubens was not primarily a portrait painter, he did many fine ones and extended portraiture into his other works,"
(30) White pointed out.

His altarpieces and paintings of heroic scope are enlivened with the "intense vitality of people you'd recognize, meet and speak with."
(35) Rubens mixed allegory and real life. A superb altarpiece includes the portrait of an archduchess, who, though for years she had worn mourning, was painted wearing an extravagant ermine robe over
(40) a luxurious satin gown accented with four long strands of 12 millimeter pearls. She kneels on the steps of the local church with great billowing curtains overhead.

But more than trappings, the
(45) archduchess's character is defined in her face. She appears as a real person. Rubens humanized his subjects, who were often his patrons, including them in altarpieces and other major works.
(50) For such was the custom of his day. Dukes, kings, and duchesses wanted to be witnesses to the nativity scene or the raising of the cross, for instance.

With a cloud of cherubs swirling
(55) overhead, the king and queen pay homage to the heavenly host.

Rubens's strong, character-defining portraits within paintings of momentous events distinguish his work.
(60) "Portraits are his commentary on people he met as an artist and diplomat. They are quite unique for the period [17th century]," White said.

Nancy Millard, "Historian Sheds Light on Rubens and Art of Portraiture."

5. This reviewer is discussing a lecture given by
   (1) a painter named Rubens
   (2) a Ball State University professor
   (3) Edmund F. Petty
   (4) a biblical illustrator
   (5) an authority on Rubens

6. The portrait of the archduchess was included in the lecture
   (1) because she seemed so real
   (2) as an example of how Rubens included contemporary portraits in his paintings
   (3) as a commentary on Rubens's friendships
   (4) to illustrate how important royal patrons were to seventeenth century artists
   (5) because it is clearly a favorite of the reviewer

7. If Rubens were a modern artist, which of the following might you expect to find in his paintings?
   (1) kings in full armor
   (2) a food vendor and a senator
   (3) a cathedral and a landscape
   (4) a cloud of cherubs and saints
   (5) a self-portrait

8. The reviewer prepares the reader for understanding White's final comment when she suggests that
   (1) including patrons was unusual
   (2) Rubens conveyed the people's humanity
   (3) portraits were the custom
   (4) artists often included patrons
   (5) Rubens was primarily a painter of allegory

Items 9–12 refer to the following art review.

IS THERE AN ESCAPE ROUTE FOR THE SCULPTOR?

Cast resin came into its own as a medium in California in the 1960's when artists like Dewain Valentine and Peter Alexander discovered in it properties that
(5) allowed them to address paradoxes of light, space, surface, and depth. Some of resin's advantages, however, soon turned out to be limitations—not least, its decorative artificiality.

(10) Herb Elsky is among the few who have persisted with the medium. For some time, he worked to subvert the singleness of the molded form, inventing a bonding process to create complex assemblages
(15) of multiple geometric components (wedges, discs, cylinders). In an attempt to undermine resin's decorative qualities, he eventually began to employ the more "organic" imagery that forms the basis for
(20) his present work.

In the works in his recent show, Elsky has introduced such opaque additives as black and white pigment, bronze powder and aluminum dust, which both counteract
(25) the fatal prettiness of the translucent resin and open up a new range of metaphors for Elsky's combinations of artificial and natural forms. Quasi-geological evocations of rock formations, jutting outcrops and
(30) deposits, internal veins and lodes, folds and ripples in the land contrast with smooth, sculpted surfaces and finely polished finishes. The most successful works are those in which the artist
(35) abandons the bonding technique and returns to the monolith: *Green Rock Place*, a solid, singular thrust of ice-green ridges emerging from a core of rugged, rocklike substance; the more intimate *Secret*
(40) *Place*, whose gradual steps leading nowhere seem time-soothed and mysterious. Elsky has also returned to traditional sculpting tools—the hammer and chisel—to break down the resin's
(45) perfect, artificial surfaces.

An impressive wall piece added an intriguing footnote to the show. Two small plain dark "plaques," each etched with a simple geometrical motif, are symmetrically
(50) paired. The resin's surface is less glossy than usual. The piece has a cool, pictorial quality that elicits a contemplative response, suggesting a possible escape route from the medium's basic tendency
(55) towards the decorative.

Peter Clothier, "Herb Elsky at Jan Baum."

9. A main idea in this review is that
   (1) artists have given up on cast resin
   (2) Elsky's organic imagery is not suited to resin
   (3) Elsky is successfully working with a difficult medium
   (4) cast resin can now be regarded as perfect for sculpture
   (5) artificial materials can't be used for sculpture

10. If Herb Elsky continues as a sculptor, he would be most likely to
    (1) use only traditional tools
    (2) experiment with additional materials and tools
    (3) be limited to only artificial forms
    (4) try and be more decorative
    (5) use only the bonding technique he developed

11. According to the review, the major problem with cast resin as a medium for sculpture is that resin
    (1) is too hard to work with
    (2) breaks down too easily
    (3) requires a bonding technique
    (4) is too artificially beautiful
    (5) is not translucent enough

12. Which of the following is not a technique Elsky employs?
    (1) using opaque additives
    (2) using a hammer and chisel
    (3) combining natural and artificial forms
    (4) using geometric forms
    (5) creating especially glossy surfaces

Performing Arts

Directions: Choose the best answer to each item.

Items 1–4 refer to the following excerpt from a music review.

IS THIS A RISING STAR?

Alison Krauss may well be the most quiet and earnest performer ever to win the adoration of the mainstream country-music audience.

(5) Country generally likes its women to have a sassy streak. But there's Krauss, a soft-voiced, high-lonesome singer and serious fiddle player, in the top 10 of Billboard's country chart—and on its
(10) Top 200 best-selling-album chart—with mega-watt divas Shania Twain, Lorrie Morgan and Reba McEntire. They knock you back; Krauss makes you lean in.

The one-time bluegrass prodigy,
(15) now 23, had made small strides toward mainstream recognition in recent years— especially her '92 album *Every Time You Say Goodbye*. Then her melancholy duet with Shenandoah's Marty Raybon,
(20) *Somewhere in the Vicinity of the Heart*, catapulted her onto country radio this year. Suddenly everyone wanted to know who owned that tender wail.

"There's an authenticity to her voice
(25) you can't deny," says Tom Rivers, program director at WQYK-FM, the mainstream country station serving Tampa-St. Petersburg, Fla. "It may not be the loudest voice, but a lot of people say it's the purest
(30) voice they've ever heard."

Country star Alan Jackson, an early convert, concurs. "One of my band guys had one of her early albums, and I just fell in love with her voice. I'm a bluegrass
(35) fan, and she's got this natural sound. She appeals to a lot of people in the music business who are more in tune with the heart than with the commercial side."

Jackson is one of many stars who have
(40) featured Krauss in duos or on backup on his recordings. Others include Morgan, Vince Gill, Dolly Parton, Nanci Griffith, Linda Ronstadt and Emmylou Harris (herself a much-sought collaborator).
(45) And more want her. In addition to working on her next album with her longtime band, Union Station, Krauss will be a guest performer on Dwight Yoakam's next album and has just
(50) recorded her first swing tune, *Any Old Time*, for an upcoming tribute album to Jimmie Rodgers.

Her current compilation album, *Now That I've Found You: A Collection*, has
(55) sold more than 2 million copies in its 26 weeks on Billboard's country chart. It includes her remake of the Keith Whitley hit *When You Say Nothing at All*, first recorded for an album tribute to the late
(60) singer; the song became a surprise follow-up smash to the Shenandoah duet.

David Zimmerman, "Country World Heeds Her Clear Siren Song," USA TODAY.

1. The feature that separates Alison Krauss from most female country music stars is
   (1) her strong voice
   (2) her soft, pure voice
   (3) her lonesome lyrics
   (4) her serious music
   (5) her melancholy duets

2. Which of the following statements about Alison Krauss is supported by the excerpt?
   (1) She has moved from mainstream country music to bluegrass.
   (2) She is a late-bloomer in the music industry.
   (3) She does not play an instrument.
   (4) She is in demand by other country musicians to work on their recordings.
   (5) She hasn't made a successful record.

3. Based on the review, which of the following phrases does not accurately describe Alison Krauss?
   (1) popular with her audience
   (2) recognized early for her talent
   (3) motivated by profit
   (4) willing to collaborate
   (5) well-liked by her peers

4. Based on this review, the reviewer appears to
   (1) know a lot about country music
   (2) know little about bluegrass
   (3) have little respect for female singers
   (4) know only mainstream country music
   (5) prefer sassy female singers

Items 5–8 refer to the following excerpt.

WHAT DOES MOST NEW MUSIC LACK?

It was 75 heavenly degrees in Miami when I left the New Music America festival December 10 and flew to New York's first deadly cold spell of the year to hear
(5) Meredith Monk and Nurit Tilles at Town Hall. They made me glad I did. Attendance at the festival was the highest in six years, but each night the numbers declined. It's not that there wasn't good music (more
(10) detail next week), but aside from Naná Vasconcelos and Lou Harrison's Third Symphony, little of the music bothered to do what Meredith Monk does best: communicate. Watch an audience dutifully
(15) endure some character's computer-hindered guitar improv; then watch Monk, doing something just as weird, zip her energy into a crowd's psyche with such superconductive efficiency that they leap
(20) to their feet and yell when she finishes. You'll suddenly realize what most new music lacks.

Monk opened with a string of solo songs, whimsical streams of humming,
(25) glissandi, nonsense syllables, and tongue clicks whose utter simplicity would have embarrassed any composer with pretensions. Her basic formal model, which has changed little since her 1976
(30) *Songs From the Hill*, is one every kindergartner understands: sing a little phrase, repeat it, sing a different phrase, work your way back to the first one. With that pattern she drew us into each piece,
(35) set us up, and played with our expectations. Get used to a syllable pattern, she'd drop one out and pop it in again where you least expected it. In its way, it was as profound a reduction of music to its
(40) essentials as was achieved by any major figure of the previous generation. Cage's and Lucier's paradigm is nature, Oliveros's is breathing, La Monte Young's is the sustained tone, but Monk's is the lullaby
(45) (she's recorded three explicitly so titled). If that isn't humankind's most primordial *musical* image, then why do her songs sound as though they echo across the millennia from a tone-world we
(50) subconsciously remember?

Kyle Gann, "Ancient Lullabies."

5. Which of the following is the best definition of paradigm (line 42) as it is used in this review?

    (1) song
    (2) breathing
    (3) expectation
    (4) model
    (5) concert

6. The reviewer suggests that much of Monk's ability to communicate is a result of

    (1) the simplicity of her basic musical pattern
    (2) her use of a computerized guitar
    (3) her formal musical education
    (4) the popularity of new music
    (5) her complex lyrics

7. The reviewer's reference to a kindergartner (line 31) is effective in this excerpt because

    (1) the review is directed at schoolteachers
    (2) it suggests how immature Monk's singing voice is
    (3) Monk is primarily a singer of children's songs
    (4) it prepared the reader for the idea of the lullaby
    (5) it contrasts Monk with musicians of previous generations

8. Judging by this review, which of the following types of music would the reviewer probably least enjoy?

    (1) traditional folk songs
    (2) the blues
    (3) instrumental jazz
    (4) bluegrass music
    (5) heavy metal rock and roll

Items 9–14 refer to the following dance review.

WHO IS THAT COCKY BOXER?

One of the triumphs of American Ballet Theatre's current national tour is *Everlast*, a new ballet by Twyla Tharp featuring the most invigorating male performance
(5) in years—Kevin O'Day as The Champ. O'Day was among the handful of dancers from Tharp's own modern dance company who accompanied her when she disbanded her troupe last year and signed on as
(10) an artistic associate at ABT. Although he spent a year in the Joffrey Ballet before joining Tharp's company, O'Day doesn't have the extensive technical background of a classical artist, but he has something
(15) ballet needs more than that: a charismatic masculinity rooted in his powerful dancing.

Everlast, which will be seen in Washington, D.C., and New York this spring, is a one-act Broadway musical
(20) at heart. A comic romance set in 1919, with music by Jerome Kern, it stars O'Day as a champion boxer betrothed to the heartless daughter of a scheming socialite and beloved by a sweet young fan. As
(25) he makes his way to happily-ever-after, O'Day plays The Champ as suitor, cocky boxer, good old pal and, at last, newly awakened lover—a range he portrays entirely and vividly in dance terms. From
(30) his introspective solos to his sparring sessions, The Champ is an authentic ballet hero. A big athletic performer with a fearless attack, O'Day commands the stage with dignity, yet his highly charged
(35) dancing has the rhythmic subtlety of a cat.

Laura Shapiro, "Where Are All the Men?"

9. Which of the following best describes O'Day's dancing?

   (1) delicately technical
   (2) gracefully vigorous
   (3) overly athletic
   (4) intentionally comic
   (5) classically rooted

10. It can be inferred from this passage that
    (1) O'Day wasted his time in the Joffrey Ballet
    (2) there are not many powerful male dancers in ballet
    (3) O'Day studied cat movements to prepare for this ballet
    (4) Twyla Tharp didn't recognize O'Day's talents
    (5) *Everlast* is too dated to be popular

11. Which of the following would be the best title for this passage?

    (1) A Return to the Days of Romance
    (2) Why Ballet is for Women
    (3) A New Hero for the Ballet
    (4) Why Twyla Tharp Abandoned Modern Dance
    (5) How the Champ Gets the Girl

12. Throughout this passage, the author is probably trying

    (1) to promote ticket sales for *Everlast*
    (2) to provide a better understanding of modern dance
    (3) to remind the reader of the value of ballet
    (4) to suggest that ballet can be quite masculine
    (5) to suggest that classical training is no longer important to a dancer

13. According to the review, the story of the ballet

    (1) is about a lonely boxer
    (2) has no likable women characters
    (3) has a happy ending
    (4) tells the history of boxing
    (5) gives a realistic picture of 1919

14. Which of the following statements about Twyla Tharp can be inferred form this review?

    (1) Her own dance company was a failure.
    (2) She only works with dancers who are technically trained.
    (3) She is interested in presenting only ballets with contemporary stories.
    (4) Her ballets are all about sports.
    (5) She is a successful ballet choreographer.

Answers begin on page 98.

# Simulated GED Test A

Interpreting Literature and the Arts

Directions

The Interpreting Literature and the Arts Simulated Test consists of excerpts from classical and popular literature and articles about literature or the arts. Each excerpt is followed by multiple-choice questions about the reading material.

Read each excerpt first and then answer the questions that follow. Refer to the reading material as often as necessary in answering the questions.

Each excerpt is preceded by a "purpose question." The purpose question gives a reason for reading the material. Use these purpose questions to help focus your reading. You are not required to answer these purpose questions. They are given only to help you concentrate on the ideas presented in the reading material.

You should spend no more than 65 minutes answering the 45 questions on this test. Work carefully, but do not spend too much time on any one question. Do not skip any items. Make a reasonable guess when you are not sure of an answer. You will not be penalized for incorrect answers. When time is up, mark the last item you finished. This will tell you whether you can finish the real GED Test in the time allowed. Then complete the test.

Record your answers to the questions on a copy of the answer sheet on page 109. Be sure that all required information is properly recorded on the answer sheet.

To record your answers, mark the numbered space on the answer sheet that corresponds to the answer you choose for each question on the test.

Example:

It was Susan's dream machine. The metallic blue paint gleamed, and the sporty wheels were highly polished. Under the hood, the engine was no less carefully cleaned. Inside, flashy lights illuminated the instruments on the dashboard, and the seats were covered by rich leather upholstery.

The subject ("It") of this excerpt is most likely

(1) an airplane
(2) a stereo system
(3) an automobile
(4) a boat
(5) a motorcycle

① ② ● ④ ⑤

The correct answer is "an automobile;" therefore, answer space 3 would be marked on the answer sheet.

Do not rest the point of your pencil on the answer sheet while you are considering your answer. Make no stray or unnecessary marks. If you change an answer, erase your first mark completely. Mark only one answer space for each question; multiple answers will be scored as incorrect. Do not fold or crease your answer sheet.

When you finish the test, use the Correlation Chart on page 73 to determine whether you are ready to take the real GED Test, and, if not, which skill areas need additional review.

Adapted with permission of the American Council on Education.

Directions: Choose the best answer to each item.

Items 1–5 refer to the following excerpt from a short story.

WHO WAS FRIGHTENED BY A KNOCK AT THE DOOR?

The footsteps came on inexorably, turned out of the road onto the graveled walk, then proceeded quickly and resolutely to the front door. First there was a light, insistent
(5) knock, then the latched screen door was heavily shaken.

"He must have a force with him," Minta thought, "he is so bold," and waited for the crash of splintering boards, and braced her
(10) body for the thrust of cold steel that would follow. She thought fleetingly of Clenmie, and of her father and mother, and wondered if any sudden coldness about their hearts warned them of her plight.

(15) The screen door shook again, and a woman's voice, old and quiet, called out, "Is there anyone home?" and ceased.

Slowly, cautiously Minta crept to the living room, lifted the side of the green
(20) blind. Old Mrs. Beal, her Sunday black billowing in the wind, was homeward bound from dinner with her daughter.

"I saw it was old Mrs. Beal on her way home from her daughter's," she told her
(25) *father, giving him as much truth as she thought he could handle.*

"Minta, you can get to the door fast enough when some of your friends are calling."

(30) *"I was busy," replied Minta with dignity. Her father looked at her doubtfully, but he said no more.*

Her mother combed out Clenmie's soft, white hair with her rhinestone back
(35) *comb. "Did you forget to feed Brownie?" she asked.*

"Of course I fed Brownie. I'll never forget her. She's my dearest friend."

Against the warm reality of Mrs. Beal's
(40) broad, homeward-bound back, the world that had been cold and full of danger dissolved. The dear room; her books, her papers; Clenmie's toys; Mother's tissue cream on top of the piano;
(45) the fire sending its lazy red tongue up the chimney's black throat.

She stood warming herself, happy and bemused, like a prisoner unexpectedly pardoned. Then she heard again the click,
(50) click she had not recognized. Brownie at the back door!

Jessamyn West, "A Child's Day."

1. What is suggested by the last sentence in this excerpt?

   (1) that Minta was hard of hearing
   (2) how much Minta loved her pet
   (3) that Minta really had forgotten Brownie
   (4) that Minta was afraid of Brownie
   (5) how much of a liar Minta was

2. What is the effect of putting part of this excerpt into italics (lines 23–38)?

   (1) The reader can see into Minta's past.
   (2) The reader is able to see into Minta's future.
   (3) What Minta imagines her future to be is made clear to the reader.
   (4) The reader understands why Minta was so cautious about Mrs. Beal.
   (5) It emphasizes how busy Minta was.

3. The "thrust of cold steel" (line 10) that Minta braces herself for refers to

   (1) the opening door
   (2) the unlatching of the screen
   (3) a piercing bullet
   (4) a stabbing knife
   (5) the fear in Minta's heart

4. The inexorable footsteps (line 1) belong to
   (1) a burglar
   (2) a group of forceful men
   (3) Mrs. Beal
   (4) Mrs. Beal's daughter
   (5) a woman in trouble

5. What effect does the sight of Mrs. Beal's back have on Minta?
   (1) She feels lonely.
   (2) She begins to worry about her father and Clenmie.
   (3) She is no longer afraid to be alone in the house.
   (4) She starts to get cold.
   (5) Her world becomes dangerous.

Items 6–11 refer to the following excerpt from an article.

HOW DID WE EVER GET INTO SPACE?

Will faster-than-light travel be possible? My inclination is to say "No," though I know it is unwise to be too categorical in such things. Back in 1928, Edward E. Smith
(5) wrote "The Skylark of Space," the first story of interstellar travel using faster-than-light speeds. He invented the inertialess drive, which is probably impossible and which, in any case, would only achieve
(10) light-speed, nothing more. Still, the principle remains.

What kind of mind is required to think of things to come to a generation and more ahead? Nothing unusual, judging by
(15) my own. It's a matter of knowing science and technology and the way they have developed, and of thinking what the next steps might logically be—and thinking and thinking. People expect dramatic
(20) shortcuts, but it boils down to the dull, hard work of thought.

Which doesn't mean that science fiction writers have anticipated everything. Their record isn't that good.
(25) For instance, they concentrated on space flight under direct human control and never realized what could be done by remote-controlled probes. They foresaw computers but missed their true role in
(30) space flight. No one, for example, predicted the advent of the microchip, the computer's compactness and versatility, and how essential it would become to piloting, say, a shuttle.

Isaac Asimov, "Truth Isn't Stranger Than Science Fiction, Just Slower."

6. According to the article, Edward E. Smith was probably
   (1) a rocket scientist
   (2) a space-flight technician
   (3) a computer expert
   (4) an astronaut
   (5) a science fiction writer

7. According to this excerpt, Asimov believes
   (1) scientific advances are always predicted in science fiction
   (2) faster-than-light travel is possible
   (3) only a genius can anticipate the future
   (4) there is an intellectual relationship between science fiction and science fact
   (5) science fiction writers know nothing about the way science really works

8. What does Asimov see as the major flaw of the "inertialess drive" (lines 7–8)?
   (1) It is clearly impossible.
   (2) It won't lead to interstellar travel.
   (3) It was invented by Edward E. Smith.
   (4) It was invented too early for true space technology.
   (5) It would only reach the speed of light.

9. Why does this passage begin with the question "Will faster-than-light travel be possible?" (line 1)?
   (1) to prepare for an explanation of interstellar travel
   (2) as a link between fact and imagination
   (3) to introduce a scientific discussion
   (4) so the author can argue against it
   (5) as an example of where science fiction writers fail

10. When Asimov says "It is unwise to be too categorical" (line 3), he means that one should not

    (1) believe what can't be seen
    (2) classify things
    (3) be too organized
    (4) deny something absolutely
    (5) make a list of qualities

11. It can be inferred from this excerpt that Asimov

    (1) disapproves of most science fiction writers
    (2) thinks that science is more important than science fiction
    (3) reads a lot of science fiction
    (4) has never written science fiction himself
    (5) has little imagination

Items 12–17 refer to the following poem.

WHO IS GOING WHERE?
Even As I Hold You

Even as I hold you
I think of you as someone gone
far, far away. Your eyes the color
of pennies in a bowl of dark honey
(5) bringing sweet light to someone else
your black hair slipping through my fingers
is the flash of your head going
around a corner
your smile, breaking before me,
(10) the flippant last turn
of a revolving door,
emptying you out, changed,
away from me.

Even as I hold you
(15) I am letting you go.

Alice Walker, "Even As I Hold You."

12. When the poet writes "as someone gone far, far away" (lines 2–3), she is preparing the reader for

    (1) the image of the bowl of honey
    (2) the idea of a revolving door
    (3) a major tragedy
    (4) a bitter parting
    (5) the last line of the poem

13. Which of the following emotions is the poet probably trying to portray?

    (1) bitter anger
    (2) solemn indifference
    (3) grateful relief
    (4) loving regret
    (5) unequaled joy

14. Which of the following subjects would this poet be most likely to write about in other poems?

    (1) the brutal nature of human beings
    (2) the beauty of a landscape
    (3) understanding in human relationships
    (4) the horrors of war
    (5) the glories of war

15. Why does the speaker describe the other person's hair, eyes, and smile?

    (1) Those are what attracted her to the person in the first place.
    (2) They are what the reader expects to read about.
    (3) They are simple to describe.
    (4) She's thinking about how other lovers will see these things.
    (5) They are all symbols of leaving.

16. The speaker is talking to someone whose eyes are

    (1) looking away
    (2) brown
    (3) blue
    (4) shut
    (5) sad

17. The speaker in this poem is probably

    (1) getting ready to leave
    (2) in love with someone else
    (3) totally unselfish
    (4) regretting her decision
    (5) preparing herself for being alone

Items 18–23 refer to the following excerpt from a play.

WHY DID JESSIE ORDER A CASE OF SNOWBALLS?

JESSIE: We got any old towels?
MAMA: There you are!
JESSIE: *(holding a towel that was on the stack of newspapers)* Towels you
(5)   don't want anymore. *(picking up Mama's snowball wrapper.)* How about this swimming towel Loretta gave us? Beach towel, that's the name of it. You want it? *(Mama shakes her head no.)*
(10) MAMA: What have you been doing in there?
JESSIE: And a big piece of plastic like a rubber sheet or something. Garbage bags would do if there's enough.
MAMA: Don't go making a big mess, Jessie.
(15)   It's eight o'clock already.
JESSIE: Maybe an old blanket or towels we got in a soap box sometime?
MAMA: I said don't make a mess. Your hair is black enough already.
(20) JESSIE: *(continuing to search the kitchen cabinets, finding two or three more towels to add to her stack.)* It's not for my hair, Mama. What about some old pillows anywhere, or a foam cushion
(25)   out of a yard chair would be real good.
MAMA: You haven't forgot what night it is, have you? *(holding up her fingernails.)* They're all chipped, see? I've been waiting all week, Jess. It's Saturday
(30)   night, sugar.
JESSIE: I know. I got it on the schedule.
MAMA: *(crossing to the living room)* You want me to wash 'em now or are you making your mess first? *(looking at the
(35)   snowball.)* We're out of these. Did I say that already?
JESSIE: There's more coming tomorrow. I ordered you a whole case.
MAMA: *(checking the TV Guide)* A whole
(40)   case will go stale, Jessie.
JESSIE: They can go in the freezer till you're ready for them. Where's Daddy's gun?
MAMA: In the attic.
JESSIE: Where in the attic? I looked your
(45)   whole nap and couldn't find it anywhere.

Marsha Norman, *'Night Mother.*

18. The stage directions in this scene suggest that the conversation is taking place primarily
(1) in the attic
(2) at night
(3) in a kitchen
(4) at the beach
(5) in a living room

19. If Jessie were to tell Mama something very unusual, how would Mama probably react?
(1) She would listen carefully.
(2) She would give Jessie only some of her attention.
(3) She would be shocked.
(4) She would go up to the attic and get the gun.
(5) She would get angry.

20. Why does the author have Jessie look for towels, plastic, a pillow, and a gun?
(1) to suggest how untidy Jessie is
(2) as a contrast to Mama eating snowballs
(3) to show how she prepares for Saturday nights
(4) because she is going to dye her hair
(5) to make the audience wonder what Jessie is planning to do

21. In which of the following ways does the author set up the relationship between these two women?
(1) through a statement in the stage directions
(2) by having them argue
(3) by having them carry on what are almost two separate conversations
(4) by revealing how much Mama is concerned about being out of snowballs
(5) by having the two directly say how they feel about each other

66   Simulated Test A

22. What does Jessie usually do for Mama on Saturday nights?
    (1) dye her hair
    (2) buy her more desserts
    (3) take her out on the town
    (4) redo her fingernail polish
    (5) get a new TV Guide

23. It can be inferred from this excerpt that Mama
    (1) is quite attractive
    (2) is fairly lazy
    (3) misses her husband
    (4) wants to go to bed soon
    (5) is a patient person

Items 24–28 refer to the following excerpt from a novel.

WHAT IS THIS MAN PROUD OF?

He loved the land no more than the bank loved the land. He could admire the tractor—its machined surfaces, its surge of power, the roar of its detonating
(5) cylinders; but it was not his tractor. Behind the tractor rolled the shining disks, cutting the earth with blades—not plowing but surgery, pushing the cut earth to the right where the second row of disks cut it and
(10) pushed it to the left; slicing blades shining, polished by the cut earth. And pulled behind the disks, the harrows combing with iron teeth so that the little clods broke up and the earth lay smooth. The driver
(15) sat in his iron seat and he was proud of the straight lines he did not will, proud of the tractor he did not own or love, proud of the power he could not control. And when that crop grew, and was harvested, no
(20) man had crumbled a hot clod in his fingers and let the earth sift past his fingertips. No man had touched the seed, or lusted for the growth. Men ate what they had not raised, had no connection with the bread.
(25) The land bore under iron, and under iron gradually died; for it was not loved or hated, it had no prayers or curses.

John Steinbeck, *The Grapes of Wrath*.

24. Which of the following best describes the activity of the man in this excerpt?
    (1) harvesting the grain
    (2) performing surgery
    (3) plowing a field
    (4) admiring the earth
    (5) touching the earth

25. What is suggested by the comparison in the first sentence?
    (1) The bank loves the land more than the man does.
    (2) The man cares very much about the land.
    (3) Both the man and the bank see the land as a source of income.
    (4) The man borrowed heavily from the bank in order to pay for the land.
    (5) Both the man and the bank have emotional investments in the land.

26. What is meant by the word iron (line 25) in the last sentence?
    (1) the seat of the tractor
    (2) the tractor and other farm machines
    (3) the iron fist of the driver
    (4) the farmer's strength
    (5) the metal deposits in the field

27. Why does the author end the passage with "for it was not loved or hated, it had no prayers or curses" (lines 26–27)?
    (1) to suggest that the land is impersonal
    (2) to explain why the man felt as he did about the land
    (3) to suggest that a person must be emotionally involved in order for the land to thrive
    (4) to suggest that farmers don't need to either pray or curse to raise good crops
    (5) to reveal that the tractor driver was not religious

28. Which of the following words best expresses this man's attitude toward the crop that will be planted?
    (1) love
    (2) hatred
    (3) greed
    (4) admiration
    (5) indifference

Simulated Test A   67

Items 29–34 refer to the following excerpt from a poem.

WHAT HAPPENED LONG AGO?

Annabel Lee

It was many and many a year ago,
In a kingdom by the sea,
That a maiden there lived whom you may know
By the name of ANNABEL LEE;
(5) And this maiden she lived with no other thought
Than to love and be loved by me.

I was a child and *she* was a child,
In this kingdom by the sea:
But we loved with a love that was more than love—
(10) I and my ANNABEL LEE;
With a love that the winged seraphs of heaven
Coveted her and me.

And this was the reason that, long ago,
In this kingdom by the sea,
(15) A wind blew out of cloud, chilling
My beautiful ANNABEL LEE;
So that her high-born kinsman came
And bore her away from me,
To shut her up in a sepulchre
(20) In this kingdom by the sea.

The angels, not half so happy in heaven,
Went envying her and me—
Yes!—that was the reason (as all men know,
In this kingdom by the sea)
(25) That the wind came out of the cloud by night,
Chilling and killing my ANNABEL LEE.

Edgar Allan Poe, "Annabel Lee."

29. The special nature of the "love that was more than love" (line 9) is emphasized by
   (1) the fact that the lovers were children
   (2) the envy of the angels
   (3) the tragedy of Annabel Lee's death
   (4) the lovers' royalty
   (5) the chilling wind that separated the pair

30. Based on the tone of this poem, the speaker will most likely
   (1) forget about Annabel Lee
   (2) murder Annabel Lee's kinsman
   (3) attend church regularly
   (4) continue to mourn his lost love
   (5) visit Annabel Lee's family

31. If Annabel Lee had survived her chill, she would most likely have then
    (1) gone home to her family
    (2) decided to become a nurse
    (3) become the speaker's devoted wife
    (4) become very religious
    (5) decided to be an independent woman

32. What is the poet's primary method for setting the mood in this poem?
    (1) referring to the wind
    (2) capitalizing Annabel Lee's name
    (3) putting the tragedy in the past tense
    (4) repeating "a kingdom by the sea"
    (5) making the cause of death unknown

33. Which of the following is suggested about the speaker?
    (1) He never looks back.
    (2) He has forgotten Annabel Lee's name.
    (3) He is not affected by life's sorrows.
    (4) He is ready for another relationship.
    (5) He still loves Annabel Lee.

34. The sepulchre (line 19) is most probably
    (1) a prison
    (2) a shallow hole
    (3) an elaborate tomb
    (4) a haunted castle
    (5) an open casket

Items 35–40 refer to the following book review.

WHY WAS THIS MAN IN THE COLD WAR?

In his heyday, between 1925 and 1945, Paul Robeson was a celebrated singer and actor and prominent symbol of the country's hopes for racial progress. But
(5) today, Robeson is perhaps best known as a cold war martyr—an outspoken admirer of Soviet communism who refused to disavow his political convictions despite a decade of government harassment.
(10) In this first major biography of Robeson, historian Martin Duberman draws on a rich array of manuscripts and interviews. A modern-day Renaissance man—he was an All-America football player at Rutgers,
(15) an actor in Eugene O'Neill's plays, a star in "Showboat"—Robeson in the '20s and early '30s hobnobbed with the smart set in New York, London, and Paris. That all changed after he went to Moscow in 1934
(20) to discuss making a film with director Sergei Eisentein. The Soviet Union bowled him over. "Here I am not a Negro but a human being," declared Robeson. "Here, for the first time in my life, I walk in full
(25) human dignity." Proud to call himself "a rigid Marxist," Robeson publicly defended every twist and turn in communist policy. The Soviet Union under Stalin he once compared to a football team: "The coach
(30) tells you what to do and we do it." Robeson eventually paid dearly for his convictions: in a sad American parody of Soviet injustice, he became a prisoner in his own land in the 1950's when the
(35) State Department denied him a passport because of his political beliefs, an action the Supreme Court ruled unconstitutional in 1957.
Duberman calls Robeson's life "*the*
(40) *American tragedy writ large.*" But that is only half the story. For what Duberman also has given us in this fine biography is also the communist tragedy writ large: a pathetic tale of talent sacrificed, loyalty
(45) misplaced, and idealism betrayed.

Jim Miller, "An American Tragedy."

35. Which of the following is true according to this review?
    (1) Robeson was killed in a war.
    (2) No major biographies of Robeson were published before Duberman's.
    (3) Robeson went unrecognized throughout his life.
    (4) Robeson moved to the Soviet Union.
    (5) Stalin was an avid football fan.

36. If Paul Robeson had been born thirty years later, he would probably have been
    (1) less outspoken in his political convictions
    (2) an actor in Eisentein's films
    (3) unknown as an actor or singer
    (4) a supporter of the civil rights movement
    (5) betrayed by the Soviet Union

37. Which of the following famous people would Robeson probably have <u>most</u> admired?
    (1) Adolf Hitler
    (2) Cesar Chávez
    (3) Queen Elizabeth II
    (4) Ronald Reagan
    (5) Carl Sandburg

38. What does the reviewer mean when he uses the phrase a "tragedy writ large" (line 40)?
    (1) that Robeson's story is a major example of a human problem
    (2) that belief in communism will lead to failure and despair
    (3) that Robeson's entire life was tragic
    (4) that one political system will often parody another's injustice
    (5) that Robeson was wrong to admire Soviet communism while living in America

39. What happened to Robeson because he openly supported communism?

    (1) He was put in prison.
    (2) He lost his self-respect.
    (3) His contract with Eisenstein fell through.
    (4) He was no longer allowed to leave the United States.
    (5) He lost his talent.

40. Why was Robeson more impressed with the Soviet Union than with the United States?

    (1) Moscow offered better career opportunities.
    (2) The Soviet Union reminded him of London and Paris.
    (3) The Communist policy encouraged individual creativity.
    (4) In the United States he felt trapped by racial prejudice.
    (5) He was following the Marxist fashion of the smart set.

Items 41–45 refer to the following excerpt from a review of a TV program.

WHY WAS THE STUDIO PACKED?

"How much time do I have?" he says.
"Two minutes," comes a voice.
He proceeds to take a cigar offered by a young man and be stunned by the number
(5) of people in this crowd from Alabama. He is relaxed and amiable.

For many of the 200 people sitting in the studio and for millions more at home, Letterman has become a generation's
(10) symbol. It's not hard to imagine any number of master's theses exploring Letterman's appeal—scholars not only of television but of society and culture as well, icon-hunting.

(15) Earlier this year, a *Rolling Stone* writer exploded thusly: "The America [Letterman] talks about is dumb (*stupid* in Letterman-speak); it is sublime. He revels in Americans; he is mad at Americans. He is
(20) the captivated, furious observer of the wild framed portrait that is American television—he has watched it closer than you and I, and it drives him crazy. So he fights with American inertia, stick by stick
(25) of furniture, guest by guest. This is how David Letterman has chosen to come into the Nineties. It's a nutty, crazy, Oval Office kind of thing."

Whew...But everybody tries to capture
(30) David.

"Letterman's playing to an audience that loves to see the world stood on its head," writes *Playboy*.

"Hip, irreverent, self-parodying, both
(35) scornful of and fascinated by the clichés of show business," writes *Time*.

Some of that is true, but the qualities one observes in a short encounter with David Letterman may come closer to
(40) defining his appeal. He's bright, quick, friendly, funny, and frank.

Rick Kogan, "Stupid Emcee Tricks."

41. The phrase "wild framed portrait" (lines 20–21) describes

    (1) an actual TV set and picture
    (2) the medium as a whole
    (3) the TV industry
    (4) a picture on a wall
    (5) the concept of TV

42. According to this review, which word best describes David Letterman in front of a studio audience?

    (1) nervous
    (2) speechless
    (3) explosive
    (4) calm
    (5) stupid

43. The reviewer calls Letterman a "generation's symbol" (lines 9–10) because the talk show host

    (1) is very funny
    (2) likes people from the South
    (3) makes fun of silliness on TV
    (4) has been the subject of master's theses
    (5) loves Americans

44. The reviewer believes that some magazine comments about Letterman

    (1) capture his personality exactly
    (2) are written by people who don't like the man personally
    (3) are understated
    (4) are completely untrue
    (5) ignore the basic reason for his popularity

45. The quotations from the magazines are used by the reviewer

    (1) to justify being a Letterman fan
    (2) to criticize Letterman
    (3) to explain Letterman's popularity in Alabama
    (4) to explain why Letterman gets into fights on his show
    (5) as examples of efforts to define Letterman's personality

Answers begin on page 101.

Analysis of Performance: Literature and the Arts Simulated Test A

Name: _____ Class: _____ Date: _____

The chart below will help you determine your strengths and weaknesses in reading comprehension and in the areas of popular literature, classical literature, and commentary.

Directions

Circle the number of each item that you answered correctly on the Simulated GED Test A. Count the number of items you answered correctly in each column and row. Write the amount in the <u>total correct</u> space of each column and row. (For example, if you answered 22 popular literature items correctly, place the number 22 in the blank before <u>out of 23</u>.)

Test A Analysis of Performance Chart

Item Types:	Literal Comprehension	Inferential Comprehension	Application	Analysis	Total Correct
POPULAR (Unit 1) Fiction Nonfiction Poetry Drama	3, 4 7, 8, 10 16 18	1, 5 6, 11 17 22, 23	13, 14 19	2 9 12, 15 20, 21	____ out of 23
CLASSICAL (Unit 2) Fiction Nonfiction Poetry Drama	24, 26 34	25, 28 33	30, 31	27 29, 32	____ out of 11
COMMENTARY (Unit 3) Literature TV and Film	35, 39 41	40 43, 44	36, 37	38 42, 45	____ out of 11
Total Correct	____ out of 13	____ out of 13	____ out of 7	____ out of 12	Total correct: ____ out of 45 (1–36 = Need More Review) (37–45 = Congratulations! You're Ready for the GED)

If you answered fewer than 37 questions correctly, determine which areas are hardest for you. Go back to the *Steck-Vaughn GED Literature and the Arts* book and review the content in those specific areas.

In the parentheses under the heading, the units tell you where you can find specific instruction about that area in the *Steck-Vaughn GED Literature and the Arts* book. Also refer to the chart on page 3.

Simulated GED Test B

Interpreting Literature and the Arts

Directions

The Interpreting Literature and the Arts Simulated Test consists of excerpts from classical and popular literature and articles about literature or the arts. Each excerpt is followed by multiple-choice questions about the reading material.

Read each excerpt first and then answer the questions that follow. Refer to the reading material as often as necessary in answering the questions.

Each excerpt is preceded by a "purpose question." The purpose question gives a reason for reading the material. Use these purpose questions to help focus your reading. You are not required to answer these purpose questions. They are given only to help you concentrate on the ideas presented in the reading material.

You should spend no more than 65 minutes answering the 45 questions on this test. Work carefully, but do not spend too much time on any one question. Do not skip any items. Make a reasonable guess when you are not sure of an answer. You will not be penalized for incorrect answers. When time is up, mark the last item you finished. This will tell you whether you can finish the real GED Test in the time allowed. Then complete the test.

Record your answers to the questions on a copy of the answer sheet on page 109. Be sure that all required information is properly recorded on the answer sheet.

To record your answers, mark the numbered space on the answer sheet that corresponds to the answer you choose for each question on the test.

Example:

It was Susan's dream machine. The metallic blue paint gleamed, and the sporty wheels were highly polished. Under the hood, the engine was no less carefully cleaned. Inside, flashy lights illuminated the instruments on the dashboard, and the seats were covered by rich leather upholstery.

The subject ("It") of this excerpt is most likely

(1) an airplane
(2) a stereo system
(3) an automobile
(4) a boat
(5) a motorcycle

① ② ● ④ ⑤

The correct answer is "an automobile;" therefore, answer space 3 would be marked on the answer sheet.

Do not rest the point of your pencil on the answer sheet while you are considering your answer. Make no stray or unnecessary marks. If you change an answer, erase your first mark completely. Mark only one answer space for each question; multiple answers will be scored as incorrect. Do not fold or crease your answer sheet.

When you finish the test, use the Correlation Chart on page 86 to determine whether you are ready to take the real GED Test, and, if not, which skill areas need additional review.

Adapted with permission of the American Council on Education.

Directions: Choose the best answer to each item.

Items 1–5 refer to the following excerpt from a short story.

WHAT'S SO SPECIAL ABOUT JEROME?

She looked in the pockets of the black leather jacket he had reluctantly worn the night before. Three of his suits, a pair of blue twill work pants, an old gray sweater
(5) with a hood and pockets lay thrown across the bed. The jacket was sleazy and damply clinging to her hands. She had bought it for him, as well as the three suits: one light blue with side vents, one gold
(10) with green specks, and one reddish that had a silver imitation-silk vest. The pockets of the jacket came softly outward from the lining like skinny milktoast rats. Empty. Slowly she sank down on the bed
(15) and began to knead, with blunt anxious fingers, all the pockets in all the clothes piled around her. First the blue suit, then the gold with green, then the reddish one that he said he didn't like most of all, but
(20) which he would sometimes wear if she agreed to stay home, or if she promised not to touch him anywhere at all while he was getting dressed.

She was a big, awkward woman, with
(25) big bones and hard rubbery flesh. Her short arms ended in ham hands, and her neck was a squat roll of fat that protruded behind her head as a big bump. Her skin was rough and puffy, with plump molelike
(30) freckles down her cheeks. Her eyes glowered from under the mountain of her brow and were circled with expensive mauve shadow. They were nervous and quick when she was flustered and darted
(35) about at nothing in particular while she was dressing hair or talking to people.

Her troubles started noticeably when she fell in love with a studiously quiet schoolteacher, Mr. Jerome Franklin
(40) Washington III, who was ten years younger than her. She told herself that she shouldn't want him, he was so little and cute and young, but when she took into account that he was a schoolteacher,
(45) well, she just couldn't seem to get any rest until, as she put it, "I were Mr. and Mrs. Jerome Franklin Washington the third, *and that's the truth!*"

Alice Walker, "Her Sweet Jerome."

1. Which of the following pairs of fairy tale characters would most resemble Jerome Washington and his wife?

    (1) Hansel and Gretel
    (2) Beauty and the Beast
    (3) Prince Charming and Snow White
    (4) The Wolf and Little Red Riding Hood
    (5) Prince Charming and the Evil Queen

2. Given the information in this excerpt, which of the following is the most likely outcome for this couple?

    (1) They will live happily ever after.
    (2) Jerome will fall in love with the woman.
    (3) The relationship will end unhappily.
    (4) The couple will adopt children.
    (5) The woman will become a schoolteacher.

3. Jerome's taste in clothing is probably

    (1) worse than the woman's
    (2) in agreement with the woman's
    (3) very loud and flashy
    (4) different than the woman's
    (5) dependent on his profession

4. Apparently Jerome will occasionally do what the woman wants him to if

    (1) she is very good to him
    (2) she buys him more clothes
    (3) she will leave him alone
    (4) she gets a better education
    (5) promises to marry him

5. According to this excerpt, which of the following is not true about the woman?

    (1) She is a hairdresser.
    (2) Her eyes move around a lot.
    (3) She is in love with a schoolteacher.
    (4) She is ten years older than Jerome.
    (5) She has found what she is looking for.

Items 6–11 refer to the following excerpt from an essay.

WHERE HAVE THE STUDIES GONE WRONG?

Robert Woodson of the Center for Neighborhood Enterprise makes the point this way: "Say you have a group of youngsters who are trying to learn to play
(5) the drums. You could study all the kids in the school who had tried and failed to learn to play the drums, observe what they were doing wrong, and then try to use your observations to help your youngsters
(10) avoid the same mistakes. Or you could focus on the kids who had learned to play the drums correctly and tell your youngsters 'This is how you do it.'"

"You cannot learn to produce success by
(15) studying failure. The only reason to spend your time studying failure is if you want to produce more failure."

Woodson was talking about something that is dear to his heart: the strengths, the
(20) resources, the success models that exist in even the most problem-ridden communities. It amazes him, he said, that we will spend enormous amounts of time and money studying the pathology
(25) of these neighborhoods while ignoring such successful drummers as Kimi Gray, who, as resident manager, has turned her Northeast Washington public-housing complex into a model of efficiency,
(30) cleanliness and resident pride. Rental collections at Kenilworth Courts are so far above the citywide average that the project not only pays its own way but actually returns a surplus to the city.
(35) "It's a mystery to me," says Woodson, "why we spend so much time analyzing our failures and so little time trying to learn from our successes."

William Raspberry, "We Can Learn Little by Studying Failure."

6. Why does the author use extensive quotations from Robert Woodson?

(1) Woodson is an expert with strong opinions.
(2) It saves a lot of explanation.
(3) The author plans to disagree with Woodson.
(4) They provide examples of his point.
(5) They give Woodson much needed publicity.

7. Which of the following is a simple definition for pathology (line 24)?

(1) a way to follow
(2) what is wrong with something
(3) the layout of an area
(4) the strength of something
(5) a model for studying

8. Why does the author call Kimi Gray a "successful drummer" (line 26)?

(1) because she makes a living with her drums
(2) because she plays the drums correctly
(3) to reinforce the analogy made in the first paragraph
(4) to suggest that musicians can become good managers
(5) to illustrate the study of failures

9. Which of the following examples might the author use to illustrate how we are "analyzing our failures" (lines 36–37)?

(1) a study of unemployment among teenagers
(2) a study of successful job applicants
(3) interviews with published writers
(4) interviews with straight-A students
(5) histories of cities that have rejuvenated their downtowns

10. It can be inferred from this excerpt that when social agencies conduct studies about failures, they not only waste their own time but also
    (1) waste the public's money
    (2) make valuable discoveries
    (3) embarrass the people they interview
    (4) waste the time of agencies that study successes
    (5) help the failures they study

11. According to this excerpt, the city where Kenilworth Courts is located
    (1) loses money on all its public-housing projects
    (2) gets money back because people at that project pay their rent regularly
    (3) gets extra money because of donations from Kimi Gray
    (4) thinks of Kimi Gray as an average resident manager
    (5) doesn't have enough public-housing complexes

Items 12–17 refer to the following poem.

WHY WAS THIS WOMAN LOOKING AT ONIONS?
Conjoined *a marriage poem*

The onion in my cupboard, a monster, actually
two joined under one transparent skin:
each half-round, then flat and deformed
where it pressed and grew against the other.

(5) Do you feel the skin that binds us
together as we move, heavy in this house?
To sever the muscle could free one,
but might kill the other. Ah, but men
don't slice onions in the kitchen, seldom see
(10) what is invisible. We cannot escape each other.

Judith Minty, "Conjoined *a marriage poem*."

12. The speaker calls the onion a <u>monster</u> (line 1) because it

    (1) frightens her
    (2) reminds her of a fairy tale
    (3) is abnormal
    (4) is hiding behind the cabinet door
    (5) is too large for the dish she is making

13. Which of the following best describes the feeling expressed in stanza two?

    (1) a cook's anger
    (2) a family's affection
    (3) a wife's frustration
    (4) a housekeeper's satisfaction
    (5) a young woman's delight

14. When the speaker refers to severing "the muscle" (line 7), she is talking about

    (1) cutting herself while slicing onions
    (2) separating the onion from its skin
    (3) killing herself
    (4) cutting dinner short
    (5) breaking the bond between husband and wife

15. The speaker says "We cannot escape each other" (line 10) because

    (1) the house is too small for much privacy
    (2) she doesn't approve of divorce
    (3) she feels that a connection holds them together
    (4) she believes in a two-income household
    (5) her husband won't give her the car keys

16. The onion described in the first stanza serves

    (1) as a symbol of harmony
    (2) to soften the tone of the poem
    (3) as a metaphor for the speaker's troubled marriage
    (4) as an image that would appeal to the reader
    (5) to demonstrate that marriage is a natural state

17. The poet includes the lines about men in the kitchen in order to

    (1) suggest that the kitchen is a woman's domain
    (2) make the reader laugh
    (3) suggest that men should do more cooking
    (4) explain why the speaker can't escape
    (5) suggest that men are unwilling to deal with emotional issues

Items 18–23 refer to the following excerpt from a play.

WHAT ARE THESE TWO DOING IN BILOXI?

DAISY: Well, if you could learn to march, you can learn to dance.

EUGENE: Yeah, except if I didn't learn to march, I'd be doing push-ups till I (5) was eighty-three.

DAISY: I'm not that strict. But if it makes you that uncomfortable I won't intrude on your privacy. It was very nice meeting you. Goodbye. *(She starts to walk away.* (10) *She gets a few steps when* EUGENE *calls out)*

EUGENE: Okay!

DAISY: Okay what?

EUGENE: One two, one two.

(15) DAISY: Are you sure?

EUGENE: Positive.

DAISY: Good. *(She walks over to him, then stands in front of him and raises her left arm up and right arm in position* (20) *to hold his wrist)*

EUGENE: All I have to do is step into place, right?

DAISY: Right. *(He tucks his cap in his belt and then steps into place, taking her* (25) *hand and her waist and he starts to dance. It's not Fred Astaire but it's not too awkward)* You're doing fine. Except your lips are moving.

EUGENE: If my lips don't move, my feet (30) don't move.

DAISY: Well, try talking instead of counting.

EUGENE: Okay...Let's see...My name is Gene. *(Softly)* One two, one two...Sorry.

DAISY: It's okay. We're making headway. (35) Just plain Gene?

EUGENE: If you want the long version, it's Eugene Morris Jerome. What's yours?

DAISY Daisy!

EUGENE: Daisy? That's funny because (40) Daisy's my favorite character in literature.

DAISY: Daisy Miller or Daisy Buchanan?

EUGENE: Buchanan. *The Great Gatsby* is one of the all-time great books. Actually, (45) I never read *Daisy Miller*. Is it good?

DAISY: It's wonderful. Although I preferred *The Great Gatsby*. New York must have been thrilling in the twenties.

EUGENE: It was, it was...That's where I'm (50) from...Well, I only saw a little of it from my baby carriage, but it's still a terrific city...What else?

DAISY: What else what?

EUGENE: What other books have you read? (55) I mean, you don't just read books with Daisy in the title do you?

DAISY: No, I like books with Anna in the title too. *Anna Karenina...Anna Christie.* That was a play by O'Neill.

(60) EUGENE: *Eugene* O'Neill. Playwrights named Eugene are usually my favorite...Listen, can we sit down? I've stepped on your toes three times so far and you haven't said a word. You (65) deserve a rest. *(They sit)* I can't believe I'm having a conversation like this in Biloxi, Mississippi.

Neil Simon, *Biloxi Blues*.

18. When Eugene says "One two, one two" (line 14) as Daisy is walking away, he is

(1) counting her steps
(2) practicing his dancing
(3) agreeing to dance with her
(4) making fun of Daisy's dancing
(5) doing push-ups

19. It can be inferred from this excerpt that Eugene is

(1) an excellent dancer
(2) a playwright
(3) an experienced flirt
(4) in the army
(5) very shy

20. Most of the stage directions in this scene are

(1) about what is happening in the background
(2) to show how Daisy and Eugene are supposed to move
(3) to demonstrate why Daisy wanted to dance
(4) too complex to follow
(5) unnecessary

21. The two have a long talk about their names because

    (1) they are both named after famous people
    (2) they are interested in how people get their names
    (3) it is a way to start a conversation
    (4) they are seriously interested in literature
    (5) all other topics of conversation have been exhausted

22. In this scene, the author is probably trying to make the audience

    (1) feel sorry for Daisy
    (2) laugh at the couple
    (3) believe in fate
    (4) sit on the edge of their seats
    (5) want to get up and dance themselves

23. If Daisy and Eugene meet again, they probably will

    (1) feel very awkward
    (2) fall into each other's arms
    (3) not speak at all
    (4) be cold but polite
    (5) be friendly

Items 24–29 refer to the following excerpt from a book.

HAVE FOLKTALES BEEN AROUND LONG?

Many and varied are the conditions favorable to the telling and hearing of folktales. In Europe they were once as important in the life of the court as among
(5) the common peoples. Kings had their story-tellers and gave them rewards and honor. Even outside of courts many men, especially in the Orient, have made a profession of telling tales and have thus
(10) earned their living. The coffeehouse is a favorite place for these Oriental raconteurs, but many other places and occasions have been used by other tellers of folktales to carry on their art. By the
(15) fireside in the evening after work the peasant loves to hear stories—and even uses them, like a young child, to go to sleep by. During working hours also the story-teller has been important in the
(20) spinning room and in the nursery; and all over the world the rest periods of shepherds, woodchoppers, fishermen, sailors, and soldiers have been favorite times for listening to tales.

Stith Thompson, *Studying the Folktale*.

24. Which is the best meaning for raconteur (line 12)?

    (1) listener
    (2) Oriental
    (3) folktale
    (4) story-teller
    (5) peasant

25. According to this excerpt, folktales have been used primarily

    (1) as bedtime stories
    (2) as entertainment
    (3) as art forms
    (4) to impress court officials
    (5) to instruct small children

26. This passage is told

    (1) in the first person
    (2) from the point of view of the story-teller
    (3) from the view of the listener
    (4) by an eyewitness
    (5) by a scholarly researcher

27. Although the telling of folktales has come to be replaced by the telling of jokes, in which situation today are folktales still more appropriate?

    (1) in a coffeehouse
    (2) after work
    (3) when putting a child to sleep
    (4) at a dinner party
    (5) during break period

28. Which of the following would be the best title for this excerpt?

    (1) A King's Favorite Tale
    (2) The Meaning of a Folktale
    (3) How to Tell a Good Story
    (4) A Cure for Insomnia
    (5) A Story for One and All

29. It is implied here that folktales are

    (1) told in different languages and about different cultures
    (2) now unpopular
    (3) about princes and princesses and dragons
    (4) much different than fairy tales
    (5) highly moralistic

Items 30–34 refer to the following excerpt from a play.

IS SILENCE REALLY GOLDEN?

GWENDOLEN: The fact that they did not follow us at once into the house, as any one else would have done, seems to me to show that they have some (5) sense of shame left.

CECILY: They have been eating muffins. That looks like repentance.

GWENDOLEN: *(after a pause)* They don't seem to notice us at all. Couldn't (10) you cough?

CECILY: But I haven't got a cough.

GWENDOLEN: They're looking at us. What effrontery!

CECILY: They're approaching. That's very (15) forward of them.

GWENDOLEN: Let us preserve a dignified silence.

CECILY: Certainly. It's the only thing to do now.

(20) *(Enter JACK followed by ALGERNON. They whistle some dreadful popular air from a British Opera.)*

GWENDOLEN: This dignified silence seems to produce an unpleasant effect.

(25) CECILY: A most distasteful one.

GWENDOLEN: But we will not be the first to speak.

CECILY: Certainly not.

Oscar Wilde, *The Importance of Being Earnest.*

30. Why does Gwendolen want Cecily to cough?

    (1) to prepare for being silent
    (2) so that Jack will think she is ill
    (3) to attract the men's attention
    (4) because the men are looking their way
    (5) to clear the muffin crumbs from her throat

31. For what purpose does the author have Jack and Algernon whistle?

    (1) to show how musical they are
    (2) as evidence of their poor taste
    (3) to fill some time
    (4) to demonstrate how casual they are
    (5) to annoy the audience

32. By having Cecily say "They have been eating muffins" (line 6), the author probably intended

    (1) the audience to take her seriously
    (2) to suggest that muffin eating shows repentance
    (3) to show how insensitive Jack and Algernon are
    (4) to suggest the time of day
    (5) to make the audience laugh

33. Given the characters of Gwendolen and Cecily, what will probably happen next in this scene?

    (1) The four will sit in silence.
    (2) Jack and Algernon will have to beg forgiveness.
    (3) Gwendolen will be the first to speak.
    (4) The women will immediately leave the room.
    (5) Cecily will burst into tears.

34. Details in this excerpt suggest that all four characters are members of the

    (1) English upper class
    (2) working class
    (3) British opera company
    (4) same breakfast club
    (5) British Parliament

Items 35–39 refer to the following excerpt from an article.

WHAT DOES CRANE SEE IN A TREE?

While some artists paint timeless pastoral scenes, Gregory Crane, 37, has invented an ingenuously quirky style of American primitive. His panoramas seethe
(5) with life of the moment—funny little pointy trees, scuttling puffs of clouds, odd tumbledown shacks. "I always responded to landscape," says Crane, who grew up in Washington state and now divides his time
(10) between Brooklyn, N. Y., and southern Vermont. Though his landscapes don't have figures in them, they have a human presence in the objects and small buildings they contain. Recently, says Crane, "I'm
(15) getting into more intimate, closed-in spaces. I've been doing more backyards." Thus, he painted *Mike and Anne's Garden in 1987.* "I like drastic shifts in scale," says Crane, explaining the juxtaposition of the looming
(20) poplar trees and the small blue structure in the background. The painting started with a small oil-and-tempera sketch that he made *en plein air* in his brother-in-law's backyard ("I don't deal with photographs,"
(25) he says). He painted the picture later in his Brooklyn studio. "I like being removed from the scene and figuring it out from my memory and information in the sketch," says Crane. Though the artist sees nature
(30) as animated ("Backyards are like portraits," he says), much of the work's liveliness is due simply to the vigorous, expressive way he paints. The pictures have a strong sense of immediacy. "I allude to the fragility
(35) of nature—a tree bent with age, a structure of this era," he explains. "I deal with the fact that we're in this apocalyptic time."

Cathleen McGuigan, "Transforming the Landscape."

35. *En pleine air* (line 23) probably means that Crane made the sketch

   (1) up from memory
   (2) with an airbrush
   (3) in his Brooklyn studio
   (4) outdoors
   (5) from a photograph

36. Which of the following quotations from the review best explains why Crane doesn't paint figures?

   (1) "I'm getting into more intimate closed-in spaces."
   (2) "I like drastic shifts in scale."
   (3) "I don't deal with photographs."
   (4) "Backyards are like portraits."
   (5) "I allude to the frailty of nature."

37. The reviewer shows how Crane "has invented an ingenuously quirky style of American primitive" (lines 2–3) by

   (1) explaining that Crane responds to landscape
   (2) contrasting his work to timeless pastoral scenes
   (3) immediately providing the reader with descriptive images
   (4) referring to the human presence in paintings
   (5) saying that his paintings contain objects and buildings

38. When the reviewer refers to the liveliness (line 31) and immediacy (line 34) of Crane's paintings, she is

   (1) linking her conclusion to her introduction
   (2) suggesting that Crane's paintings are too vigorous
   (3) commenting on the fragility of nature
   (4) rephrasing Crane's own remarks
   (5) referring to the shifts in scale

39. The most probable meaning of the word animated (line 30) as it is used here is

   (1) cartoonlike
   (2) alive
   (3) factual
   (4) cluttered
   (5) stiff

Simulated Test B

Items 40–45 refer to the following review.

WHAT MAKES SOMEONE A MAGICIAN?

Magician David Copperfield has levitated a 750-pound motorcycle, a Ferrari and even himself. He made the Statue of Liberty vanish, pop bands and
(5) jets, so it was a little surprising when he called that the phone didn't float just a little bit above the table. But Copperfield doesn't work on long-distance phone lines, and it takes months to prepare the
(10) performances. The magician plans and plots each act of prestidigitation, many of which leave his fans gasping in amazement.

"Everybody has a love affair with the unknown," Copperfield said of his audience's
(15) fascination with his breathtaking illusions.

"People want to escape in a fantasy for a while. The more sophisticated the audience is, the greater their desire to escape."

Copperfield, who will perform shows at
(20) 5:30 p.m. and 8:30 p.m. today at Clowes Hall at Butler University, makes everybody marvel at his magic.

"I demonstrate in my shows that everything I do in the TV specials, like
(25) the *Escape From Alcatraz*, can be done onstage. In my new show, I will do a self-levitation and levitate a motorbike. I also will escape from the Death Saw, a performance which is very dangerous,"
(30) Copperfield said.

To make every show more interesting, he approaches the performances from different angles.

"I have different styles and I choose new
(35) music. The audience should not only be amazed, but also challenged."

Copperfield did 500 live shows last year and admitted that doing performances continuously is tiring and a hard job. But
(40) the dangerous elements in his shows keep him growing.

"When you are onstage night after night, you tend to be on automatic pilot. But with the dangerous pieces I have to be aware
(45) of what I do. They actually keep me awake and concentrated."

He said that it is challenging to explore new combinations of illusions. After performing at the Bermuda Triangle, the
(50) Grand Canyon and China, Copperfield still thinks "there's a lot out there" to keep him interested in spectacular acts. He might do a TV special in Egypt.

In 1982, Copperfield founded the
(55) Project Magic, an organization that teaches magic to people with disabilities to motivate their therapy.

Magicians and therapists are working together in about 1,000 facilities all over
(60) the world.

"It's not the stuff I do, but there's an immediate satisfaction for the disabled," he said. "Magic makes the patients feel better."

Anja Freyer, "Magician Finds His Shows Hard Work."

40. According to this article, why is magic so appealing?
   (1) Magic helps cure disabilities.
   (2) Levitation can help people move things around.
   (3) People occasionally enjoy escaping from reality.
   (4) Spectators like to participate.
   (5) There is not enough real danger in life.

41. Acts such as the escape from the Death Saw enable Copperfield to
   (1) perform on automatic pilot
   (2) do more live shows each year
   (3) perform in various countries
   (4) stay more alert on stage
   (5) do more television specials

42. Which of the following activities would Copperfield probably engage in during his free time?
   (1) learning how long-distance phone calls work
   (2) donating time to a local children's home
   (3) taking a class in self-motivation
   (4) watching old television reruns
   (5) learning how to meditate

84   Simulated Test B

43. Why does the author mention her surprise that her phone didn't float?

    (1) because she really had expected it to float
    (2) to illustrate that levitation works only on large objects
    (3) to set up a difference between illusion and reality
    (4) to suggest that magicians can fail sometimes
    (5) as an example of how amazing magic is

44. This magician's live performances prove that

    (1) his TV tricks owe a lot to the camera's special effects
    (2) anything he does on TV he can do onstage
    (3) TV magic is more amazing than live magic
    (4) certain tricks are better onstage
    (5) magicians depend on simple props

45. The reviewer uses quotations from her talk with Copperfield

    (1) because she didn't quite understand what he had said on the phone
    (2) so that she wouldn't give away any of his secrets
    (3) to demonstrate his understanding of the psychology of magic
    (4) because she isn't really sure how magic works
    (5) to show how mysterious he really is

# Analysis of Performance: Literature and the Arts Simulated Test B

Name: _____ Class: _____ Date: _____

The chart below will help you determine your strengths and weaknesses in reading comprehension and in the areas of popular literature, classical literature, and commentary.

Directions

Circle the number of each item that you answered correctly on the Simulated GED Test A. Count the number of items you answered correctly in each column and row. Write the amount in the total correct space of each column and row. (For example, if you answered 22 popular literature items correctly, place the number 22 in the blank before out of 23.)

Test B Analysis of Performance Chart

Item Types:	Literal Comprehension	Inferential Comprehension	Application	Analysis	Total Correct
POPULAR (Unit 1) Fiction Nonfiction Poetry Drama	 5 7, 11 12 18, 20	 3, 4 10 14, 15 19, 21	 1, 2 9 23	 6, 8 13, 16, 17 22	 _____ out of 23
CLASSICAL (Unit 2) Fiction Nonfiction Poetry Drama	 24 	 25, 29 30, 31, 34	 27, 28 33	 26 32	 _____ out of 11
COMMENTARY (Unit 3) Visual Arts Performing Arts	 35, 39 41, 44	 38 40	 42	 36, 37 43, 45	 _____ out of 11
Total Correct	_____ out of 11	_____ out of 14	_____ out of 8	_____ out of 12	Total correct: ___ out of 45 (1–36 = Need More Review) (37–45 = Congratulations! You're Ready for the GED)

If you answered less than 37 questions correctly, determine which areas are hardest for you. Go back to the *Steck-Vaughn GED Literature and the Arts* book and review the content in those specific areas.

In the parentheses under the heading, the units tell you where you can find specific instruction about that area in the *Steck-Vaughn GED Literature and the Arts* book. Also refer to the chart on page 3.

86   Analysis Performance Test B

Answers and Explanations

UNIT 1: POPULAR LITERATURE

Fiction (pages 4–11)

1. **(4) Bert and Manny are longtime friends.** (Literal Comprehension) The text says Bert and Manny had been "friends for twenty years" (line 4). Therefore, all the other options are incorrect.

2. **(3) funeral** (Literal Comprehension) This information is given in lines 14–22. Option (2) is incorrect because Manny didn't feel any grief, although he knew he should. The other options are not supported by the text.

3. **(4) special events director** (Application) Manny is very interested in planning Bert's funeral and making it memorable. Options (1) and (3) are not likely since he displays little sympathy. Option (2) is incorrect because he doesn't indicate any interest in medicine. Option (5) is incorrect because there is no information to support his possible writing skills.

4. **(2) too excited to sleep** (Literal Comprehension) This information is given in the text. Therefore, options (1), (4), and (5) are incorrect. The mother, not Turtle, is interested in the man's bald spot (option 3).

5. **(5) a character in a pirate story** (Inferential Comprehension) This information is not stated directly but can be inferred from Taylor's use of the words "pirate" and "Captain Hook" as she thinks about Turtle's question. Option (1) is incorrect because the captain introduces himself as only "your captain." Jax (option 2) is mentioned but his last name is not given. There is no name given for the man in the next seat (option 3). There is no mention of Turtle's father (option 4).

6. **(3) They have probably flown before.** (Inferential Comprehension) This inference can be made from the statement that "Everybody else on the plane is behaving as though they are simply sitting in chairs a little too close together" (lines 51–53). There is no information to support any of the other options.

7. **(1) to live in a new place** (Inferential Comprehension) No destination is mentioned but reference to a "new life" in line 69 makes this a reasonable assumption. None of the other options are supported by the text.

8. **(5) old Luze** (Literal Comprehension) "He" also refers to himself as "old Luze." There is no basis for options (2) and (4). Option (1) is grammatically impossible. That "we" watched him wave goodbye eliminates option (3).

9. **(4) schoolchildren** (Inferential Comprehension) Old Luze has made them both promise to go back to school. Option (5) is wrong because they are ashamed of themselves, not him. There is no evidence for the other options.

10. **(1) to emphasize the suspense of waiting** (Analysis) The ideas are not complex (option 5), nor is there a reason for contrast with the dialogue (option 4) or the first sentence (option 3). Option (2) is wrong because dialogue has nothing to do with length. Option (1) refers to the tension of waiting for the train.

11. **(2) getting on the train** (Literal Comprehension) It refers to the train and snag means catch, or get on which Luze does before he waves (option 1). There is no support for options (3), (4), or (5).

12. **(2) because Lee wasn't interested in football** (Literal Comprehension) Options (1) and (4) are contradicted in the text. Option (3) has no support. Option (5) is wrong because the narrator contrasts savvy with sense. Option (2) is part of the example for this contrast.

13. **(4) Lee reminded the narrator of his youth.** (Literal Comprehension) Options (1), (2), (3), and (5) are all mentioned. There is no evidence that option (4) is true.

14. **(3) an intellectual talking bird** (Literal Comprehension) Schwartz, clearly a bird, reads to the boy and appears to have fairly refined taste. He is not a pet (option 1), is unwelcome only to the father (option 2), and is a firm tutor (option 4). He may like chess (option 5), but we don't know how much.

15. **(3) slightly fanciful** (Analysis) Options (1) and (5) are both too extreme. There is no evidence for either option (2) or option (4). The scene is almost believable.

16. **(5) a mutiny** (Inferential Comprehension) It can be inferred from the details in the excerpt that crew members have taken over a ship. Therefore, all the other options are incorrect.

17. **(2) two guns** (Literal Comprehension) This detail is given in lines 12–13. Option (1) is incorrect because it was the curtain that was blue and no mention is made of a shirt. The excerpt says specifically that the captain was not found (option 3). Option (4) is incorrect because they found one hat. The fireman in option (5) refers to a member of the ship's crew who was not in the cabin.

Answers and Explanations 87

18. **(1) Peter** (Inferential Comprehension) The action in the excerpt shows that Peter was in charge. Options (2), (3), and (4) are incorrect because all of these characters defer to Peter. Option (5) is incorrect because, while the captain might once have been in charge, he is missing.

19. **(3) bully** (Inferential Comprehension) Turno not only beats up Aaron, but taunts him as well. Therefore, he is not a weakling (option 1) or a prankster (option 2). There is no evidence for options (4) or (5).

20. **(2) a victim** (Literal Comprehension) This information is stated in the excerpt. There is no evidence for options (1) or (5). Photographs (option 3) are mentioned in the excerpt, but no photographers. The only police officer (option 5) whose name is given is Marti.

21. **(2) The police want Joe to identify some people who have been killed.** (Inferential Comprehension) Marti doesn't actually say why she is showing Joe the pictures, but it becomes clear that this is the reason. Options (1) and (3) are incorrect because the police are not interested in how Joe sells or gives away food. Option (4) is incorrect because Joe is not trying to keep anyone away. There is no photographer in the story, so option (5) is incorrect.

22. **(1) He tried to help them.** (Inferential Comprehension) Joe describes how he left food out for them to take, so he was clearly trying to help. There is no support for any of the other options.

23. **(2) an electronic game machine** (Literal Comprehension) Checker Charley is the name of the machine. Options (1), (3), (4), and (5) are wrong because they refer to people.

24. **(3) He expects to lose the game.** (Inferential Comprehension) Paul is comparing the likelihood of his winning to the sun not rising, but the sun always rises (option 1). Option (2) is the opposite of option (3). Options (4) and (5) are not true.

25. **(2) He believes he will win the money.** (Inferential Comprehension) There is no evidence for options (1), (3), or (4). Berringer would have no reason to signal Paul (option 5), but he does expect to take the money home.

26. **(5) Paul is ahead.** (Literal Comprehension) Paul is taking the checker pieces. There is no evidence for the other options.

27. **(3) confident** (Inferential Comprehension) Lines 1–11 provide details that lead to this inference. Therefore, all the other options are incorrect.

28. **(2) extremely** (Inferential Comprehension) This meaning of the term best fits the context. Therefore, all the other options are incorrect.

29. **(3) an algebra teacher** (Literal Comprehension) This is stated in the text. There is no support for options (1), (2), (4), or (5).

30. **(1) The narrator is extremely worried about a person he had once known well.** (Analysis) Options (4) and (5) are not suggested by this passage. Option (2) is wrong as the ice is not real. Option (3) is the opposite of what is stated.

31. **(3) to have changed physically because of drug use** (Inferential Comprehension) This is suggested in the last few lines. Options (1), (2), and (5) have no support in the excerpt. Option (4) is probably the opposite of reality.

32. **(2) as a vivid example of how distressed the narrator is** (Analysis) The ice is a metaphor, a comparison that helps the reader understand how the teacher is feeling. Option (1) is not true. Options (3) and (4) are irrelevant. Option (5) is unlikely.

33. **(4) regret for what Sonny once was like** (Inferential Comprehension) The narrator remembers Sonny's gentleness and the bright look on his face, and is saddened at what he has become. However, he is not disgusted (option 1) or afraid (option 2). He certainly is not relieved (option 3) or happy (option 5) that Sonny has been caught.

34. **(5) before he got to school** (Literal Comprehension) This information is given in lines 1–3. Therefore, all the other options are incorrect.

Nonfiction (pages 12–17)

1. **(2) The odds were against Marshall.** (Analysis) The writer asks what makes Marshall and his lawyers think they could "reverse the tide of segregation" (lines 3–4) and "alter the legal landscape of America" (lines 6–7). Since options (1) and (4) state the opposite, they are incorrect. The writer does not indicate he thinks there is no chance (option 3) or that both sides have an equal chance (option 5).

2. **(4) unequal pay for black teachers** (Literal Comprehension) This information is given in lines 39–40. Option (1) is incorrect because slavery had ended before Marshall's time. Option (2) is incorrect because segregation was the subject of the later case. Option (3) is incorrect because it is not mentioned and is too general. Option (5) is incorrect because states' rights were used to support segregation, the condition Marshall argued against.

3. **(5) great respect** (Inferential Comprehension) The excerpt says that as a law student Marshall cut classes to hear Davis, something he would do only if he respected Davis. He was not in awe (option 1) of Davis or he would have been afraid to go up against him in a case. Options (2) and (3) are not supported by the text. Option (4)

88 Answers and Explanations

would not account for Marshall's cutting class to hear Davis.

4. **(3) Marshall's belief in himself and his cause** (Literal Comprehension) This information is stated in line 43. Options (1) and (4) are not true. Option (2) is not mentioned. Option (5) is incorrect because Governor Byrne's actions did not help Marshall's chances.

5. **(2) He had won thirteen cases before the Supreme Court and lost only two.** (Literal Comprehension) This information is stated in lines 33–34. Options (1), (3), and (4) are not true. Although the excerpt says Byrne was paying Davis with "a silver tea service," option (5) is incorrect because no issue is made about the payment.

6. **(3) Roberto Clemente always played to win.** (Inferential Comprehension) Not only does Clemente say he always plays to win (line 47), but the point of the excerpt is to illustrate that fact. None of the other options is the overall idea of the excerpt.

7. **(2) He was a close friend of Clemente.** (Literal Comprehension) This information is stated in lines 6–7. Therefore, all the other options are incorrect.

8. **(4) He took the game seriously.** (Inferential Comprehension) Wearing his uniform meant the softball game was just as important as a big league game. Options (1) and (5) are incorrect because they imply attitudes that are not supported by the excerpt. Option (2) is not true. Option (3) is not mentioned in the excerpt.

9. **(1) intense** (Analysis) Everything in the excerpt shows that Clemente took all games seriously and always played to win. Options (2), (3), and (4) are not supported by the excerpt. Option (5) is true but not the best description.

10. **(1) his house** (Literal Comprehension) This is made clear in the text. He takes the figurative phrase literally rather than applying it to actual people as in options (2), (3), (4), or (5).

11. **(3) to defend against** (Literal Comprehension) The idea of protection is repeated here. The other options do not suggest an active protection.

12. **(2) innocent and experienced** (Inferential Comprehension) This shows the difference between the child and the adult. One half of each of the pairs in options (1), (3), and (4) is wrong. Option (5) is not a contrast.

13. **(2) that a carelessly spoken word can cause harm** (Inferential Comprehension) The whole piece is based on an overheard phrase. Although options (1) and (3) are true, they are not main ideas. Options (4) and (5) are not supported by evidence.

14. **(1) Horses usually can't do math problems.** (Inferential Comprehension) Math is usually done only by people, not other animals. There is no support for options (2), (4), and (5); and option (3), though true, is not amazing in itself.

15. **(5) Body language can communicate expectations.** (Inferential Comprehension) All of the options are true, but only option (5) includes all of the possibilities.

16. **(4) paying even closer attention to the audience** (Application) As a man, Hans would be aware of the audience's contribution to his act and would probably take advantage of the fact. Magic (option 1) and calculus problems (option 2) would be secondary to observation. Options (3) and (5) would hinder, not help, the performance.

17. **(2) to emphasize the scientific validity of the discovery** (Inferential Comprehension) These words are associated with thinking, especially scientific thinking. There is no evidence for options (1), (3), or (5). No one is absolutely sure what the basis for spoken language is (option 4).

18. **(4) Children don't want to earn their own livings.** (Literal Comprehension) All of the other options are mentioned in the text.

19. **(2) to bring the reader back to the idea in the first paragraph** (Analysis) Envision refers back to visualize, the concept of being able to see what work is. It is not evidence (option 1) of anything or a contrast (option 4) to anything. Option (3) is wrong because modern jobs are comprehensible to most adults. There is no support for option (5).

20. **(1) In most families, only the father works.** (Analysis) All the examples are about men. No working women or mothers are mentioned. Options (2) and (4) are not what the author says or implies. Options (3) and (5) are incorrect because the author doesn't say old jobs were better or more satisfactory, but rather that they were easier for children to understand.

21. **(2) state an opinion about jobs** (Analysis) The author gives information and examples only to support his opinion about today's jobs. Option (1) is incorrect because the author's purpose is not primarily to give facts about jobs. Option (3) is incorrect because the author uses questions merely as a device to make his point. Options (4) and (5) are not true since the author gives neither type of information.

22. **(5) abstract** (Analysis) Details given in the excerpt describe jobs that cannot be explained or seen and understood. Therefore, all the other options are incorrect.

Answers and Explanations

23. **(2) rough** (Literal Comprehension) Living in the open is rough. There is no support for the other options.

24. **(2) fascinated** (Analysis) Although the author is obviously impressed by Snowbird, awed (option 1) is too strong a word. He does not pity the man (option 3), and probably would find nothing to feel confused (option 4) or sad about (option 5).

25. **(3) read the sights and sounds of nature** (Inferential Comprehension) Although option (1) may be true, it is not suggested here. Option (2) is not true. Options (4) and (5) are not supported by evidence. In option (3), read means to interpret.

26. **(4) to sum up Snowbird's world view** (Analysis) The quotation does reveal how Snowbird thinks. Option (1) is poor because a quotation doesn't prove that he knew Snowbird. Option (2) is wrong because a quotation isn't needed to state a simple fact. Options (3) and (5) are not relevant to the quotation.

27. **(3) short** (Literal Comprehension) The excerpt says Snowbird was "five feet tall" (line 5). None of the other options are true.

28. **(1) He is eager to continue living and learning.** (Inferential Comprehension) Snowbird says he is "just beginning to grow" (line 33). This statement makes option (1) the only possible choice. Each of the other options contradicts his words.

Poetry (pages 18–26)

1. **(4) grief** (Analysis) The entire poem conveys overwhelming sadness at the death of a loved one. Options (1), (3), and (5) are not supported by the poem. Although the speaker does express anger, it is part of her grief.

2. **(2) own feelings that are still raw** (Inferential Comprehension) These lines imply a comparison of the raw, exposed wood to the still raw emotions the speaker has been expressing throughout the poem. There is no support for any other option.

3. **(5) biting into a piece of candy** (Literal Comprehension) Lines 11–12 make the comparison of the log to "a chocolate nougat." Option (1) is incorrect because no mention is made of an oak tree. The comparisons in options (2) and (3) are used in the poem but not to refer to cutting into the beech log. Option (4) is not part of a comparison in the poem.

4. **(2) a loved one** (Inferential Comprehension) The speaker says "You are four months dead." The mood of the poem and all of its images imply that the speaker has lost someone she loved very much. Option (1), (3), and (5) are not possible because the speaker would not feel a sense of loss about a stranger, a distant relative, or an enemy.

Option (4) is incorrect because details such as "your old cigarette cough" clearly imply an adult.

5. **(4) a man writing to his newborn granddaughter** (Inferential Comprehension) Options (1), (3), and (5) are wrong because the speaker in the poem wrote these words (line 18), rather than spoke them. Although we are given no clue as to the speaker's gender, we do know the child's name is Emily (the poem's title), that she might grow up to be a mother (line 15), and that she is "two generations away" (line 2), making the speaker a grandparent, so options (2) and (5) are wrong.

6. **(2) fifty-three** (Literal Comprehension) This information is stated in line 3. Option (1) refers to the child's future, and options (3) and (4) refer to the speaker's future.

7. **(3) Love endures.** (Inferential Comprehension) Options (1) and (5) may be true, but they are not suggested in the poem. Option (2) is suggested in the poem but only as an example of the main idea. Option (4) goes beyond the information provided in the poem. Option (3) is supported by the poet's emphasis on love and is essentially a paraphrase of lines 15 and 16.

8. **(3) know about this poem** (Literal Comprehension) In line 13 the speaker says that Emily will have read her children the poem. Option (1) is incorrect because it is the opposite of what the speaker says in line 12. Option (2) is contradicted by the poem. There is no evidence in the poem for options (4) or (5).

9. **(5) He didn't like his work.** (Inferential Comprehension) Option (1) is suggested by the too in line 1. Options (2) and (3) are supported by weekday weather in line 4. Option (4) is supported by lines 3 and 4. Only option (5) has no support in the poem.

10. **(3) warmth and cold** (Analysis) Although all options are mentioned in the poem, the repeated images of warmth and cold emphasize the warmth of the father's love contrasted with the son's cold indifference.

11. **(2) the father's dutiful care of the family** (Analysis) The simple but lonely task of lighting the fires was done out of love. Options (1) and (5) refer to the son, but he was not the one who loved. Option (3) refers to an opposite emotional climate. Option (4) is wrong, being based on necessity, not love.

12. **(4) He regrets his thoughtless lack of understanding.** (Inferential Comprehension) The last two lines of the poem suggest that the poet has finally come to understand the value of his father's love. Options (1), (2), and (3) are the opposite of this, and option (5) has no support.

13. **(2) the fire was warming the rooms** (Inferential Comprehension) Since line 7 says "when the rooms were warm," it makes sense to conclude that line 6 is figurative language describing the effect of the fire warming the cold rooms. Nothing in the poem supports any of the other options.

14. **(1) The boy would go to church.** (Inferential Comprehension) The references in the poem to "Sundays" (line 1) and "polished my good shoes" (line 13) lead to the inference that the boy would be going to church. Options (2) and (3) are incorrect because there is no school or work on Sunday. Option (4) is not likely because this is not something we would expect this father to do. Option (5) is incorrect because "offices" in the last line doesn't refer to a place.

15. **(3) A person has been shot in the city.** (Literal Comprehension) The gender of the body is not specified, but the details of the setting—trees, streets, utilities—suggest the city rather than the country (option 2). There is no support for options (1), (4), or (5).

16. **(1) It implies a casualness to the killing.** (Analysis) The lifting of a cigarette is an ordinary and casual act, not one that would bring violence to mind (option 4). Option (2) is wrong because the phrase is a metaphor, not a description of reality. Although options (3) and (5) might be suggested, the emphasis is on the act itself.

17. **(3) by repeating several key words** (Analysis) Options (2), (4), and (5) have no support. While option (1) may represent an aspect of death, it would be the following phrase that would serve to emphasize. The repetition of closed, forever, and abandoned serves to focus the reader on finality.

18. **(4) get a second job** (Application) Crow is acting out of the need for survival; basic needs must be met before emotional reactions can be important. Options (1), (2), (3), and (5) focus on emotion.

19. **(5) Crow** (Analysis) Crow arrived too late to save someone very important to him. Nothing in the poem supports the other choices.

20. **(2) Life must go on.** (Application) Crow must go on living even though his grief is profound. Option (1) is not supported by the poem. Although the last line refers to finding something to eat, that is just the immediate step Crow must take; therefore, the meaning of option (3) is too narrow. The poem doesn't address whether Crow survived because he was fit (option 4) and the person who died wasn't. Since hope is not conveyed by the poem, option (5) is incorrect.

21. **(3) a bare old table** (Literal Comprehension) The plates the couple eat from rest on wood. Plain suggests unfinished. The creaking would be a result of age. Options (1), (2), and (4) don't meet all these requirements. Option (5) meets only the age requirement.

22. **(5) die poor but happy** (Application) Options (1) and (3) are not suggested in the passage. Both options (2) and (4) are contradicted by the twinkling (line 10), the pleasure of remembering.

23. **(3) to show the wealth of the couple's memories** (Analysis) Options (1) and (2) would be the mark of an inferior poet. The additional line helps to describe the simple but treasured things that have created good memories, not battered remnants (option 4) or a tidy house (option 5).

24. **(2) as evidence of the couple's way of life** (Analysis) Unusual capitalization serves to point out a significant feature. Here, rather than giving details of the couple's lives, the poet classifies them and follows with an example in lines 7 and 8. For the most part, they do what they should but are not saints (option 4). There is no support for options (1), (3), and (5).

25. **(3) They are surrounded by reminders of their lives.** (Inferential Comprehension) Lines 11–13 give examples of items that they have collected during their lives. Option (1) is not supported by the poem. Options (2) and (4) are the opposite of what the poem implies. Option (5) may be true but is not relevant.

26. **(2) They remember both good and bad times.** (Inferential Comprehension) "Twinklings" implies happy memories and "twinges" implies regret or guilt. Option (1) is incorrect because the couple remembers their past. Options (3) and (4) imply incorrectly that they are having to seach for something. Option (5) is not implied in the poem.

27. **(4) a street address** (Inferential Comprehension) A street address can appear on a front gate, and that is the best explanation for the reference here. There is no evidence in the poem for options (1), (2), and (3). Option (5) is incorrect because a ZIP Code would not logically be on a gate.

28. **(2) her nose** (Literal Comprehension) This information is stated in the poem (lines 20–21). All the other items were painted, but not because of an itch; therefore, they are incorrect.

29. **(4) the posts** (Analysis) All the other options are things that would not normally be painted, even option (3), which she explains in line 13.

30. **(3) lighthearted** (Analysis) There is no support for options (1) or (2). Option (4) is too strong a word. Option (5) is not accurate because the speaker is laughing at herself.

31. **(3) Blue is the color associated with the post office.** (Inferential Comprehension) There is no real support for the other options, but the

Post Office, which uses mailboxes, is associated with the color blue. Option (5) is clearly wrong given the speaker's happy mood.

32. **(2) make enough for ten people** (Application) The speaker tends to get carried away and do things in excess. Options (1), (3), and (5) suggest more discipline than the speaker seems to have. There is no support for option (4).

33. **(1) A Refuge for a Child** (Application) There is no support for options (4) and (5). Although the child may be getting away (option 2) or may love nature (option 3), neither reflects her need for thought.

34. **(5) a novice nun in a convent** (Application) The child is seeking thoughtful solitude, not the company of other people (option 1) or creative energy—as implied by options (2), (3), and (4). A young nun would probably have some of the same motives for retiring from the world.

35. **(2) under a bush** (Inferential Comprehension) The description of branches, blooms, and leaves suggest a large shrub. Options (1), (3), and (4) are incorrect because they are figurative descriptions of the space under the shrub. Therefore, option (5) is incorrect.

36. **(4) she likes to think and dream** (Inferential Comprehension) The poem describes Lisa sitting comfortably, lost in her own thoughts. Her brothers (option 1), dogs (option 2), and a bicycle (option 3) are described as part of the scene of which she is unaware. Option (5) is incorrect because she is "lost" only in thought.

37. **(3) the sky** (Inferential Comprehension) This descriptive language refers to the pieces of the sky that show through as the clouds part. Therefore, the other options are incorrect.

38. **(3) Each time you look at the sky, it is different.** (Analysis) The repeated phrase illustrates looking at the sky but seeing it differently each time. Options (1) and (2) are not supported by the details in the poem. Option (4) is incorrect because the poem says the sky is "colder than," not the same as a frozen river. Option (5) is incorrect because the poem is not about time.

39. **(4) is inspired by nature** (Inferential Comprehension) The speaker is so moved by this aspect of nature that she wants to express it. Options (1) and (5) may be true, but they are not referred to in the poem. Option (2) appears to be untrue since the speaker doesn't complain about the cold. Option (3) seems unlikely since the poem is written for students.

40. **(4) frogs** (Literal Comprehension) This information is given in lines 34–37. The other options are incorrect because they name things the speaker says she is not afraid of.

41. **(1) to show that the speaker is trying to sound brave** (Analysis) The speaker is trying to convince herself and everyone else by repeating that she is not afraid. Option (2) is incorrect because this is a common childish behavior, not bragging. Option (3) is incorrect because it wrongly implies that the speaker is confused. There is no support in the poem for options (4) and (5).

42. **(2) a young girl** (Inferential Comprehension) Lines 29–33 imply that the speaker is a girl, and both the language and content of the poem suggest that she is young. Therefore, all the other options are incorrect.

Drama (pages 27–31)

1. **(2) are old friends** (Inferential Comprehension) Although never stated directly, it's clear from the conversation that the two women have known each other for many years. Therefore, options (1), (3), and (4) are incorrect. Option (5) is incorrect because both women seem to be enjoying the conversation.

2. **(3) She thinks Gina looks foolish.** (Inferential Comprehension) Maggy ridicules Gina's appearance on the float. Therefore, option (1) is incorrect. Option (2) is incorrect because Maggy doesn't seem to have a high opinion of Robbie Bigelow. Options (4) and (5) are incorrect because they are contrary to what is stated or implied in the conversation.

3. **(4) talks a lot** (Application) Based on her behavior in this situation, it is reasonable to assume that Maggy will be talkative in other similar situations. Options (1), (2), and (3) seem unlikely based on the excerpt. Option (5) is incorrect because Maggy seems to enjoy conversations with friends.

4. **(3) pretending he is like the man in his play** (Literal Comprehension) This information is given in Bing's speech (lines 13–14). Options (1) and (5) refer more to his play. Neither options (2) nor (4) are true.

5. **(4) A O K** (Application) A O K could be seen as the phrase for approval: A-Okay. Options (1), (2), and (3) would all be negative. Option (5) would have no meaning.

6. **(2) very young** (Analysis) Options (1) and (3) are wrong because Bing is not yet sure of success. There is no evidence for options (4) or (5) in this scene, but his attitude is one of youth.

7. **(3) to show how little Bing really understands about greatness** (Analysis) Bing's lack of understanding is shown through his envy of O'Neill's success, not admiration of O'Neill's abilities. He makes a faulty connection between family background and skill. Options (1) and (4) suggest the opposite. Option (2) has no

support. The *Inferno* is a poem by Dante, not O'Neill (option 5).

8. **(2) He doesn't believe he is a very good teacher.** (Literal Comprehension) There is no real evidence for options (1), (3), (4), or (5). Frank does, however, say that he is an appalling teacher and supports this idea throughout the passage.

9. **(4) You can't make a silk purse out of a sow's ear.** (Application) Frank believes that he could not be as good an instructor as Rita needs, even if he tried. He is the sow's ear and what Rita needs is the silk purse. The other options all refer to the use of time, not skill.

10. **(2) It indicates that Rita has changed her mind.** (Analysis) The contrast in Rita's attitudes suggests a decision and change in mood. There is no support for options (1), (3), (4), and (5).

11. **(1) uncertainty** (Analysis) All four of the other options appear, but only briefly, in Frank's speech. He has doubts about himself and how to present himself. He hesitates and changes the subject often.

12. **(4) He thinks he knows absolutely nothing.** (Literal Comprehension). This information is stated in lines 20–23. Options (1) and (2) are contradicted by the excerpt. Option (3) is true, but is a reason he gives for being a good teacher. Option (5) is not a reason he is a terrible teacher.

13. **(4) He was assigned as her tutor.** (Literal Comprehension) Rita says she wants him as her teacher because he was assigned to her and she doesn't want anyone else. Options (1) and (5) are not supported by the excerpt. Options (2) and (3) are not true.

14. **(4) church parish** (Inferential Comprehension) Fitzgibbon's later discussion of a church parish suggests that St. Dominic's is similar. There is no evidence for the other options.

15. **(1) a software troubleshooter** (Application) O'Malley's job seems to be to fix things that have gone wrong, not to be a planner or to promote as suggested by the other options.

16. **(1) show how friendly these men are** (Analysis) The directions indicate emotions or actions that demonstrate concern and assurance. None of the other options have support in the stage directions.

17. **(2) he is actually describing his own earlier behavior** (Analysis) Options (1), (4), and (5) are not suggested by innocently. Option (3) is wrong because the rest of the text does not support that the Father is unaware of (innocent of) how much like the other old priest he is.

18. **(3) an engaged couple** (Inferential Comprehension) Options (1), (2), (4), and (5) are unlikely because of the kiss in the elevator.

19. **(5) jealous** (Inferential Comprehension) Option (1) is not supported by Tiffany's questions. There would have been no questions if options (2), (3), or (4) were true.

20. **(4) The couple really did kiss in a cab.** (Analysis) Options (3) and (5) are not supported by the text. Option (1) may be true but is not relevant here. Tiffany's answer is a joke in itself (option 2). That the joke became reality is what is funny and ironic.

21. **(5) by arguing until she gets her way** (Application) Tiffany gives no evidence of behaving in the way described by options (1), (2), (3), or (4). She does, however, argue with Bob until he tells her what she wants to know.

22. **(4) in an elevator** (Literal Comprehension) Tiffany reminds Bob of this fact in line 10. Therefore, all the other options are incorrect.

23. **(5) he saw her smashed fingernails** (Literal Comprehension) Frank states this information in lines 28–30. Option (1) refers to Tiffany, not Mary. Options (2), (3), and (4) are events that occurred earlier in the sequence of events leading to the kiss.

UNIT 2: CLASSICAL LITERATURE

Fiction (pages 32–35)

1. **(1) Don Quixote has a vivid imagination.** (Inferential Comprehension) Don Quixote imagines that the windmills are giants he must slay. Options (2) and (4) are incorrect because, while they both are looking at the windmills, Sancho Panza only sees them literally, and Don Quixote sees them as adversaries in an imaginative adventure. Even though Don Quixote says to Sancho Panza "if you are afraid," there is no evidence that Sancho is afraid (option 3). Option (5) is incorrect because Don Quixote says he will fight the giants even though they are numerous and huge.

2. **(3) He would be unconcerned.** (Application) In this excerpt Don Quixote is ready to go against "thirty or more monstrous giants." Options (1) and (4) are incorrect because they are the opposite of what the excerpt shows about Don Quixote. Options (2) and (5) are incorrect because in this excerpt Don Quixote ignores Sancho Panza's explanation and is determined to proceed without him.

3. **(1) worried about finding an intruder in his home** (Inferential Comprehension) He is checking to make sure no one is hiding and to see that nothing has been moved. Options (2) and (5) are wrong because there is no evidence of his plans. He is clearly familiar with how and where everything should be, so options (3) and (4) are wrong.

4. **(4) Double-Checking** (Application) The passage suggests that Scrooge is nervously making sure all is in order, therefore eliminating option (5). Option (1) has no support, and there is no evidence of a city (option 2). Nothing has happened yet, so option (3) is wrong.

5. **(4) He came to see George's mother.** (Literal Comprehension) Eugene states this information in line 26. Therefore, all the other options are incorrect.

6. **(3) He didn't want his mother to know Eugene had come.** (Inferential Comprehension) Based on George's message to Eugene, it can be assumed that George knows that Eugene is at the door and wants to send him away before his mother knows Eugene has arrived. For this same reason, option (1) is incorrect. Options (2), (4), and (5) all deal with the housemaid, and there is no evidence that George's motivation for answering the door had anything to do with her.

7. **(5) He didn't expect any fuss.** (Inferential Comprehension) Although Eugene seems surprised that George answers the door, he nevertheless says why he has come and clearly doesn't expect George to reply as he does. Therefore, options (1) and (3) are incorrect. Option (2) is not indicated by anything in the text and contrary to the usual procedure of Mary answering the door. Option (4) is incorrect for two reasons: He clearly didn't expect George to answer since Mary usually did so; based on the subsequent conversation it is logical to assume that Eugene and George were not on good terms and George would not have invited Eugene in.

8. **(1) refined** (Analysis) George and Eugene speak formally and remain conventionally polite even when they get angry. Therefore, options (2), (3), and (5) are incorrect. Even though Eugene begins the encounter in a friendly manner (option 4), he soon changes in response to George who is unfriendly from the beginning.

9. **(3) Uncle Buddy is after the dogs that are chasing a fox around the house.** (Literal Comprehension) Option (1) implies that Uncle Buddy is in control of what is happening. Options (2) and (5) limit the chase to the kitchen and, along with option (4), confuse the actual order of who is chasing whom.

10. **(4) The chase had led through the woodpile by the chimney.** (Inferential Comprehension) Option (4) is supported by the sticks of firewood that get involved in the chase. There is no evidence for option (1). The noises in options (2) and (3) would not create the sound described. Option (5) suggests that Uncle Buddy would be hurt, but he isn't. Also note the word like meaning as if; nothing actually happened to the chimney.

11. **(5) part of the family** (Inferential Comprehension) Although options (1) and (4) may be true, there is no support for these two opinions. There is no evidence for option (3). The fact that there is a dog's room makes option (2) wrong and suggests that option (5) is correct.

12. **(2) putting all the action in one long sentence** (Analysis) The one long sentence builds clause on top of clause to create an impression of breathlessness. Option (1) comments on the chase, but doesn't contribute to it. No one's reactions, as suggested by option (3), are described. Options (4) and (5) are merely part of the chase.

13. **(2) a ship's horn** (Literal Comprehension) This information is stated in lines 15–16. Option (1) is incorrect because no fire is mentioned. Although a dog (option 3), a fox (option 2), and a chimney (option 5) are mentioned, they are not compared to Uncle Buddy's bellowing.

14. **(5) reciting the multiplication tables** (Literal Comprehension) "7 times 9" is part of the multiplication tables. The class is obviously reciting, so options (1) and (2) are wrong. Options (3) and (4) are wrong because these actions don't take place until afterward.

15. **(1) what the boys have learned in school** (Literal Comprehension) There is no evidence that the boys have ever heard about option (2). Option (3) reflects a confusion about the word stores. The lesson in learning was from Mr. Bhaer (option 4). These are evidently good boys and they probably rarely cheat (option 5).

16. **(3) because he realizes he already has been able to learn something** (Inferential Comprehension) Options (1) and (2) are wrong because they don't occur until after Nat decides. Options (4) and (5) are wrong because Nat doesn't believe them either, but he has learned how to be patient and how to fiddle.

17. **(5) sympathetic** (Inferential Comprehension) There is no support for options (1), (2), and (4). Although option (3) could be true, it is not the main quality that is demonstrated.

18. **(2) how well Nat played the fiddle** (Application) The reader has no way of knowing everything that Mr. Bhaer included in his "lesson in learning." However, when Mr. Bhaer had finished, we are told that the other boys warmly received Nat, "the chap who had fiddled so capitally."

19. **(2) manners** (Analysis) Options (1) and (3) are wrong because they would require a more casual but vigorous style. Options (4) and (5) are wrong because they would be written more formally and less colorfully.

Nonfiction (pages 36–38)

1. **(1) nature** (Inferential Comprehension) Although the moth is attracted by the sunlight (option 2) and is seeking his freedom (option 3), the implication is that the same source gives energy to people, animals, and even the land. There is no evidence for option (4). Moths don't feel ambition (option 5).

2. **(3) tiny** (Literal Comprehension) Part of the key lies in an implied comparison of the size of the world—large—to that of the moth. Options (2) and (5) don't apply to a physical description. Options (1) and (4) may be true but are not implied by diminutive.

3. **(2) an inability to see the obstacles in life** (Application) The window is invisible to the moth and is something it does not understand as a barrier. People often have the same problem in perceptive difficulties. The other options are either too literal (option 4) or exaggerated.

4. **(5) to suggest that the moth represents the life-force** (Analysis) The moth may be small (option 1) and insignificant (option 2), but it is filled with energy, the life-force. Options (3) and (4) are not supported.

5. **(5) It doesn't know how limited its existence is.** (Inferential Comprehension) This inference can be made from lines 8–14. Option (1) is not supported by the text. Options (2), (3), and (4) are incorrect because they express ideas opposite of those expressed in the excerpt.

6. **(5) the best-qualified person** (Literal Comprehension) This answer is provided in the last sentence of the text. There is no evidence for the other options.

7. **(2) disagreed with Sayers** (Analysis) This was a controversial topic at the time the article was written, and Sayers's opinions were not generally accepted. Therefore, all the other options are incorrect.

8. **(3) The modern home is too small.** (Literal Comprehension) This answer is stated in the text. The ideas in options (2) and (4) are suggested in the text, but not as reasons for the problem. There is no support for options (1) and (5).

9. **(4) get training and education** (Application) The author is not concerned with specific skills, as suggested by options (3) and (5), nor does she encourage giving up (option 2). Rather than urging protest (option 1), she believes that having the proper skill is the best way to get the job.

10. **(5) reasonable** (Analysis) The author is presenting a persuasive argument, using logic and evidence, not emotion. The other options are based on emotional response.

11. **(1) support gender-neutral hiring policies** (Application) This is a logical application of the author's belief that the best qualified person should have the job. Options (2), (3), and (4) are not supported by the excerpt. Option (5) is incorrect because the author uses the word if in lines 26–28 to qualify the notion of women as office workers.

12. **(3) mastering the facts of a worthy subject** (Literal Comprehension) This answer is given in the second sentence. The other options are possible results of scholarly pursuit, but do not reflect the author's intent.

13. **(3) Humans still tend to be uncivilized.** (Inferential Comprehension) Forster believes that if humanity paid attention to true scholarship, true civilized behavior would result. But as humanity is still uncivilized, he concludes that scholars have failed to influence society. Options (2) and (4) are wrong because they contradict the stated skills of the scholar. There is no support for options (1) and (5).

14. **(5) provide a well-known example of a true scholar** (Analysis) Raleigh is clearly being used as an example that would be familiar to his readers. There is no support for the other options.

15. **(2) Humanity still has a long way to go to be civilized.** (Inferential Comprehension) In the author's view, humanity is still uncivilized. Because there are few true scholars, humanity will continue to ignore the value of the relationships between facts. Options (1) and (4) are not true. Options (3) and (5) are not suggested in the passage.

16. **(5) the author** (Literal Comprehension) The author says that Raleigh once held "this lectureship" as the author himself now does. Therefore the other options are incorrect.

17. **(4) Concentrate on one subject and other subjects related to it.** (Application) This option is a logical extension of what the author says in lines 3–6. Therefore, all the other options are incorrect.

Poetry (pages 39–44)

1. **(2) The girl sings very quietly.** (Literal Comprehension) Since lines 6–7 say the vale was "overflowing with the sound," she could not have been singing quietly. All the other options are stated in the poem.

2. **(3) The speaker shifts the focus to himself.** (Analysis) The last stanza is the only one in which the speaker uses the pronoun "I" and writes about himself. Options (1) and (2) are contradicted in the poem. Option (4) is incorrect because the poet refers to his feelings about the scene with the girl singing. Option (5) is not supported by the poem.

3. **(4) This experience will remain in his memory.** (Inferential Comprehension) The speaker says the music will remain with him for a long time. Therefore, all the other options are incorrect.

4. **(3) She lived an active, happy life.** (Inferential Comprehension) All the details in the poem show Lucinda engaged actively in a life she loved. Options (1) and (2) are true but too limited to describe her life. Option (4) is not supported by the excerpt. Option (5) is contradicted by the poem.

5. **(4) later generations** (Inferential Comprehension) These lines seem to refer to young people of a later time. Although the reference could be to her own sons and daughters (option 1) or to other children (option 2), there is no evidence in the poem to suggest she was disappointed in them specifically. Options (3) and (5) do not make sense since the reference is to "sons and daughters."

6. **(1) She had an inner joy.** (Inferential Comprehension) This line and others in the poem show Lucinda's joyous approach to life. Options (2) and (3) are contradicted by the text. Options (4) and (5) are not supported by the text.

7. **(5) Work hard, but enjoy life.** (Application) Lucinda's life illustrates this philosophy. All the other options express ideas that are contrary to Lucinda's beliefs.

8. **(3) suggest that there are two speakers** (Analysis) The speaker in quotation marks is asking questions, not being quoted (option 2). The unmarked stanzas are replies by another speaker to those questions, eliminating options (1) and (4). Option (5) is wrong because all stanzas are dialogue, not description.

9. **(4) death** (Literal Comprehension) Each of the other options is dealt with by a set of two stanzas. The questions involve the living, not the dead.

10. **(5) He is dead.** (Inferential Comprehension) Line 4 provides the first clue and is reinforced throughout the poem. Sleep (line 24) for this speaker is only figurative (option 1). There is no support for options (2), (3), or (4).

11. **(3) Life, in general, continues even after an individual dies.** (Inferential Comprehension) The friend in this poem has not betrayed the dead man (option 1), nor has the woman (option 2). They have simply gone on with life. The poet is not necessarily suggesting that ghosts exist (option 4) or that he believes in the immortality of the soul (option 5); having the dead man ask questions is a device by which to explore the central question.

12. **(5) the funeral** (Literal Comprehension) The reference to the "dark parade," the funeral, is in the future tense. All of the other options are expressed in the present, as if being seen by the speaker.

13. **(2) mechanically** (Analysis) This word suggests that the people in the house are not acting in a normal way, that their emotions are temporarily on "automatic pilot." Options (1) and (3) do not have this connotation. The other options suggest distaste (option 4) or mystery (option 5), not numbness.

14. **(4) the activities of the living** (Inferential Comprehension) Horror (option 2) and distress (option 5) are not part of this poem. The observer shows no reaction (option 3), but simply says what he sees. The people described are not necessarily mourning (option 1); rather they are doing the things that must be done to bury the dead and go on with living.

15. **(4) to suggest that death is mysterious and alien to children** (Analysis) Although the speaker understands death because of his own experience (option 1), the key is in the use of pronouns. It shows how the children cannot see the dead as a person. That also underlines a distance between the children and an understanding of death. Options (2) and (5) are not as important to the children as the strangeness of death itself. Option (3) is wrong because the phrase refers to their curiosity, not their fear.

16. **(2) a man living across the street** (Inferential Comprehension) Line 1 refers to "the opposite house," and line 13 refers to when the speaker was a boy. Therefore, the other options are incorrect.

17. **(4) the undertaker** (Inferential Comprehension) Many people fear death and find the funeral business associated with it "appalling." Options (1) and (2) are incorrect because these occupations have nothing to do with death. The minister (option 3) and the doctor (option 5) are mentioned in the poem but not in the verse that refers to the "appalling trade."

18. **(3) a fall evening** (Literal Comprehension) This information is in line 6. There is no support for the other options.

19. **(1) threatening** (Literal Comprehension) Most of what is described in the first ten lines is threatening, i.e., the threat of a storm. Evil (option 2) is too strong a word. Options (3), (4), and (5) would better apply to the speaker's reactions than to the tone.

20. **(2) to suggest a striking snake** (Analysis) This is a metaphor suggesting the actions we associate with a snake. Options (1) and (5) are wrong because they do not refer to the leaves. Options (3) and (4) have no support.

21. **(4) It weakens the comfort the last line should provide.** (Analysis) This technique is called approximate rhyme and is often used to call the reader's attention to an unstated weakness or strength in the literal wording. There is no evidence for options (1), (2), or (3). Option (5) is wrong because all of the other lines in the poem use true rhyme, not just lines 13 and 15.

22. **(3) rain** (Literal Comprehension) All the other options are details mentioned in the poem.

23. **(2) He is profoundly alone.** (Inferential Comprehension) The speaker says he is so alone that he has no one left but God (lines 15–16). Options (1), (4), and (5) are incorrect because there is no evidence for them in the poem. Option (3) contradicts the last line of the poem.

24. **(1) deprived of a loved one by death** (Analysis) The tone of the poem is somber and very sad, and the speaker describes a state of being completely alone except for God. Option (1) is the only option that accounts for these factors. All the other do not explain this great aloneness.

25. **(3) They each found something.** (Literal Comprehension) Although their discoveries were different, each girl found something on the beach. Options (1), (2), and (4) are not suggested by the poem. Although option (5) might apply to three of the girls, it probably wasn't true of molly who didn't enjoy what she found.

26. **(4) molly was more easily scared than the others** (Inferential Comprehension) While the other discoveries seem somewhat magical, molly's seems frightening. But what the poet describes is a crab, not really a horrible thing. What makes it horrible is molly's own fear, the self she found in the sea. Options (1) and (3) are contradicted by evidence in the poem. There is no support for options (2) and (5).

27. **(2) It emphasizes the break between the story and the poet.** (Analysis) A poet's use of an unusual feature often indicates emphasis; in this case it emphasizes the transition between description and analysis. Option (1) is wrong because the other complete sentence is not capitalized. There is no support for options (3) or (5). Option (4) is wrong because there is no change in rhythm.

28. **(4) suggest the mysterious quality may saw in the stone** (Analysis) The two comparisons help the reader see the stone as unusual because we do not normally call a world small or think of the word alone in terms of size. Option (1) is wrong because the description is figurative, not realistic. There is no relation between the similes and the suggestions in options (2) and (3). Option (5) is wrong because, although the shell also has a mysterious quality, the similes do not compare the two objects.

29. **(5) It gives the poem a pleasing repetition of sounds.** (Analysis) Alliteration, the repetition of initial consonant sounds, is a common poetic device that can provide a pleasing effect. Option (1) is untrue. Option (2) might be true but is not significant to understanding or enjoying the poem. There is no support for option (3). Option (4) is incorrect because monotony is not a quality the poet would want in this poem.

Drama (pages 45–47)

1. **(4) implies that she alone knows what is best for Barbara** (Inferential Comprehension) Lady Britomart's belief that she alone knows what is best for people is supported throughout the excerpt. Although she might be concerned about Barbara's welfare (option 2), she doesn't show any faith in anyone else's opinion (option 3). There is no support for options (1) and (5).

2. **(4) wary of her interference** (Analysis) Stephen is wary of his mother interfering in his personal life, though he tries to hide this behind a polite exterior. Options (1), (2), (3), and (5) are not supported by the evidence.

3. **(2) He was born in Australia.** (Inferential Comprehension) All other options are mentioned as positive qualities, either directly or by implication. Option (2) is the only one that is expressed in a negative manner.

4. **(5) amusement** (Analysis) While both characters in this excerpt probably take themselves seriously, the audience will find their discussion rather funny, especially Lady Britomart's inability to see her own snobbishness. Options (1), (2), (3), and (4) would be the results of misunderstanding the play.

5. **(2) a rich man's house** (Inferential Comprehension) Support can be found in that servants can be hired, Johansson has wanted to see the house (homes of the rich are generally appealing), and dinner parties are a regular affair. Option (1) refers to Bengtsson's simile, not reality. The same is true of the ghost metaphor (option 3). There is no evidence for options (4) or (5).

6. **(1) the older faculty members** (Application) The tone of the valet's answers is that of a subordinate who feels that he knows better than those who have more authority than he. This might be the case with a graduate student. Options (2), (3), (4), and (5) refer to people that Bengtsson would feel equal or superior to.

7. **(4) unusual conversation between people** (Application) Option (1) is eliminated by the dialogue. Options (2) and (5) are unlikely, considering how peculiar the people sound. Option (3) is incorrect because it is based only on a metaphor.

8. **(5) to provide further information about the household** (Analysis) Information about the

household is provided as a result of Johansson's questioning. Option (1) is a fact, not a reason. There is no support for the other options.

9. **(2) He has never worked in this house before.** (Inferential Comprehension) Johansson has dreamed of working in this house (lines 11–12), but since this is his first evening there he must ask questions about the event. Therefore, options (1), (3), and (5) are incorrect. Option (4) is incorrect because, although he does think the people are peculiar, this doesn't keep him from wanting to work there.

10. **(4) He knows Johansson slightly.** (Inferential Comprehension) Two reasons make this option the best choice: Johansson uses the phrase "as you know" (Line 9), and Bengtsson is very willing to tell Johansson about the eccentricities of the household. Therefore, all the other options are incorrect.

11. **(3) write about everything except the assigned topic** (Application) Helena does tend to ignore the other person's remarks and tends to ramble from subject to subject. She takes herself seriously (option 4) and cannot be described as either clear (option 1), timid (option 2), or logical (option 5).

12. **(4) The Ignored Suitor** (Application) Helena ignores Voitski's remarks except when they begin to annoy her. She is not really concerned about her husband (option 3) or the environment (option 2). There is no support for options (1) and (5).

13. **(2) as a melodramatic person** (Analysis) Voitski's dialogue could be interpreted as melodramatic, as material straight from a soap opera. Options (3) and (5) imply more maturity and control than Voitski exhibits. He is not purposely being jolly (option 1) or rude (option 4).

14. **(4) Helena's statement that men have no mercy** (Inferential Comprehension) There is not enough support for options (1), (2), or (3). Option (5) is opposite to Helena's belief.

15. **(1) Helena and Voitski** (Literal Comprehension) This information is given in lines 31–34 where Helena addresses Voitski by Ivan, his first name. Therefore, all the other options are incorrect.

UNIT 3: COMMENTARY

Literature (pages 48–51)

1. **(4) She has written both fiction and nonfiction.** (Literal Comprehension) This information is given in lines 33–45. None of the other options is supported by the text.

2. **(2) as a way of coping with her grief** (Inferential Comprehension) This is a logical inference from Allende's words, "Or was I going to write a book that would heal me?" (lines 13–14) and "I could not let anger destroy me." (Lines 27–28) None of the other options can be inferred from the review.

3. **(3) consider it her fate** (Application) Since this is the attitude Allende expressed about her daughter's death (line 25), it can be assumed that she would react to her own situation similarly. Options (1), (2), and (4) are contrary to the choices she made after her daughter's illness. There is no evidence for option (5).

4. **(1) The author has a high opinion of Allende's work.** (Inferential Comprehension) The author refers to Allende as "distinguished" (line 1), and the entire review is very positive. There is no evidence to support option (2). None of the other options is addressed in the review.

5. **(5) It is generally entertaining and informative.** (Inferential Comprehension) The reviewer uses the words useful and fun to describe the book. There is no support for options (1), (2), (3), and (4).

6. **(3) that Shenkman has done his own thorough research** (Inferential Comprehension) The reviewer implies options (1), (2), (4), and (5). Option (3) is not suggested; Shenkman used other people's research.

7. **(4) saying "on the other hand, is very good" (lines 25–26)** (Analysis) The phrase in option (4) indicates a contrast to the previous statement.

8. **(5) legends and myths** (Literal Comprehension) This word is a summary of the topic that this book addresses; bunk refers back to the title, in that a significant portion of history is based on myths, lies, and legends—rather than facts. Option (2) is a different meaning of the word, not appropriate in this context. Options (1), (3), and (4) are eliminated because they are all the opposite of option (5).

9. **(2) through the experiences of individual soldiers** (Literal Comprehension) This point of view is given in the last paragraph. The Southern general (option 5) is only one of the participants. Although battle fatigue (option 4) might play a part in the men's experience, it is not the focus. There is no evidence for options (1) and (3).

10. **(5) The reality of war involves raw emotion, not logic.** (Inferential Comprehension) Logic plays a part in planning war (see first paragraph), but not on the battlefield or in the hearts of the soldiers. There is no support for options (1) and (2). Although options (3) and (4) may be part of the overall picture, they do not directly answer the question.

11. **(1) It creates a powerful basic image of the battlefield.** (Analysis) The first short words not only describe the abrupt visual impact of a battlefield but also have an internal repetition of a harsh vowel sound, followed by the strong alliteration of the repeated m. Options (2), (3), and (4) are not suggested in the text. The basic image is in opposition to option (5).

12. **(4) to suggest the extent of the general's insanity** (Analysis) Despite news of the war's possible end (option 2), the general's mind cannot accept defeat. This is not a rational decision (option 3), not even in the military (option 5). Option (1) might be in part a cause of the insanity, but not the result.

13. **(2) A policeman frequently took the place of a judge who had a hangover.** (Literal Comprehension) Option (1) is not true. There is no general evidence for options (3) or (4). Option (5) may be partially true, but is not the main idea of the paragraph.

14. **(5) bribery** (Inferential Comprehension) This is suggested by "bribe-happy gang" and the examples. Options (1) and (2) were crimes but not in the court system. There is no evidence for options (3) or (4).

15. **(4) Honesty is the best policy.** (Application) Devine was anything but honest. Options (2) and (3) both suggest taking advantage of opportunity, and Devine arranged to get money without spending much time (option 1). He also had little respect for the people with whom he worked (option 5).

16. **(3) a miracle worker** (Application) This lawyer apparently specialized in making deals for drunk drivers. The bagman (option 2) would not be as useful, since he would have to be approached through the lawyer. Neither Martin (option 1) nor Sodini (option 5) seem involved in bribery. And Operation Greylord (option 4) cleaned up the corruption.

17. **(1) Justice could be bought.** (Inferential Comprehension) The entire review focuses on bribery and corruption in the Cook County court system. All other options are contradicted by the review.

TV and Film (pages 52–55)

1. **(5) superb** (Literal Comprehension) The reviewer refers to the "greatness" of his performance (line 31). Therefore, all the other options are incorrect.

2. **(4) The reviewer is impressed with the director's skill.** (Literal Comprehension) The reviewer says the director "knows what he is doing" (lines 40–41). Therefore, options (1), (2), and (5) are incorrect. Option (3) is not supported by the review.

3. **(3) powerful** (Analysis) The sentence refers to the actor's powerful performance. None of the other options is supported by the text.

4. **(2) disconnected** (Inferential Comprehension) In line 21, the author describes how Christy speaks in separate syllables. None of the other options includes this meaning of the word.

5. **(3) a guide to good children's programs** (Inferential Comprehension) The reviewer has chosen programs that involve children or appeal to them and describes the quality of each one. Option (1) is incorrect because this is not a miscellaneous group. Options (2) and (4) are incorrect because not all of the shows are new or about animals. Option (5) is incorrect because no awards are mentioned.

6. **(4) a serious story** (Literal Comprehension) The reviewer uses the words "slapstick antics" (line 16) and other words to describe this show as a comedy. All the other options are given as features that make the show successful.

7. **(1) It is a weekly show.** (Literal Comprehension) This information is stated in line 32. Therefore, all the other options are incorrect.

8. **(2) science fiction** (Analysis) The review includes the types of programs in all the other options.

9. **(5) Frank** (Inferential Comprehension) The reviewer says the actor who plays Frank has "tried hard—though he still grates" (lines 58–59). All the other options are incorrect because the author says more positive things about these characters.

10. **(2) is insignificant** (Inferential Comprehension) The reviewer says "in some episodes her son might as well be a lamp" (line 41). Therefore, all the other options are incorrect.

11. **(5) Most episodes have weak endings.** (Literal Comprehension) Lines 21–23 state this information. Therefore, all the other options are incorrect.

12. **(3) This is an outstanding show.** (Application) Since the author says he "became a fervent fan" when the show premiered (lines 12–13) and refers to the show as "brilliant" (line 63), an earlier review would probably include this opinion. There is no evidence to support the other options.

13. **(4) a journey in search of something** (Literal Comprehension) Although the ideas of a chase (Option 2) or a trip (Option 5) are included in the word, the key is in the idea of a search. Options (1) and (3) would make no sense in this context.

14. **(1) Charlie Babbitt learning to love** (Literal Comprehension) This answer is given in the last sentence. Option (2) does not happen. Options (3), (4), and (5) are wrong because Raymond cannot change.

15. **(2) glorified outlaws** (Application) Options (1), (3), and (5) are portrayals that are generally accurate, while Option (4) is not the same type of comparison. Option (2) is based on an attempt to bring the abnormal within the understanding of the normal.

16. **(2) how far he has retreated into his own world** (Analysis) Raymond does not interact with people, so Option (1) is wrong. Option (3) refers to only one-half of the comparison. Options (4) and (5) have no support.

Answers and Explanations

Visual Arts (pages 56–58)

1. **(3) publicity and marketing techniques** (Literal Comprehension) Options (1), (2), (4), and (5) are all parts of the overall publicity and marketing techniques.

2. **(5) refuse to use computer technology** (Application) Option (5) is the only response that does not reflect Josiah Wedgwood's sharp business sense and willingness to update his facilities.

3. **(2) a variety of Wedgwood designs for modern customers** (Inferential Comprehension) Wedgwood has continued Josiah's strategy of creating new designs. There is no evidence for options (1) and (3). Options (4) and (5) are marketing techniques independent of this problem.

4. **(2) develop larger markets for their work** (Application) The trend referred to is of marketing to retailers. There is no support for options (1), (3), (4), or (5) to be the results of a trend.

5. **(5) an authority on Rubens** (Literal Comprehension) The lecturer has written books on Rubens. He is also from Oxford University (option 2). Option (3) is the occasion for the talk. Rubens, sometimes a biblical illustrator (option 4), was the subject of the talk.

6. **(2) as an example of how Rubens included contemporary portraits in his paintings** (Inferential Comprehension) The archduchess, a contemporary of Rubens, is found in an altarpiece. Option (1) refers to how Rubens humanized his subjects. Options (3) and (4) are too general. Option (5) may be true, but the reviewer is not the lecturer.

7. **(2) a food vendor and a senator** (Application) Rubens used both important people and ordinary people in his paintings. Options (1), (3), and (4) would be more likely in the 17th century. There is no support for option (5).

8. **(2) Rubens conveyed the people's humanity** (Analysis) Rubens didn't stylize his portraits, but painted people realistically, apparently an unusual practice.

9. **(3) Elsky is successfully working with a difficult medium** (Literal Comprehension) Details in the article show that Elsky is overcoming the limitations of cast resin. There is no support for options (1) or (4). Elsky's success so far implies that options (2) and (5) are wrong.

10. **(2) experiment with additional materials and tools** (Application) Elsky's willingness to experiment is pointed out, thus eliminating options (1), (3), and (5). Option (4) is wrong because that is what he has been working to avoid.

11. **(4) is too artificially beautiful** (Inferential Comprehension) In lines 9, 17, and 25, the author refers to resin in various ways that lead to this inference. None of the other options can be inferred from the information given.

12. **(5) creating especially glossy surfaces** (Inferential Comprehension) The reviewer describes the sculptor's efforts to avoid the glossy surfaces that resin produces. All the other options are techniques the sculptor does use.

Performing Arts (pages 59–61)

1. **(2) her soft, pure voice** (Literal Comprehension) Krauss's voice is referred to in this way in lines 28–29. None of the other options is supported by the excerpt.

2. **(4) She is in demand by other country musicians to work on their recordings.** (Literal Comprehension) She has appeared on recordings of other artists many times. Options (1), (3), and (5) are contradicted by the excerpt. Option (2) is incorrect because she is described as a "prodigy" (line 14).

3. **(3) motivated by profit** (Inferential Comprehension) This is implied by the statement that she "appeals to a lot of people in the music business who are more in tune with the heart than with the commercial side" (lines 37–38). All other options describe Krauss.

4. **(1) know a lot about country music performers** (Analysis) The reviewer includes a great deal of information about country music performers and their works. All the other options are contrary to the information in the review.

5. **(4) model** (Literal Comprehension) This word refers to the basic structure or pattern, a model, for each musician's musical form. Options (1), (2), (3), and (5) would make no sense in this sentence.

6. **(1) the simplicity of her basic musical pattern** (Inferential Comprehension) The reviewer devoted most of the commentary to a discussion of this simple pattern in order to explain Monk's appeal. Options (2) and (5) are not true according to the excerpt. There is no evidence for options (3) and (4).

7. **(4) it prepared the reader for the idea of the lullaby** (Analysis) The term sets up a context in which the childlike simplicity of the lullaby will be understandable. Option (2) is wrong because the reference is to the style of her singing, not to the quality of her voice. There is no evidence for options (1) and (3). Option (5) is wrong because there is no suggestion of contrast or comparison at this point.

8. **(5) heavy metal rock and roll** (Application) The reviewer seems to enjoy music with repeated patterns and a fairly universal appeal, qualities more common to the first four options than to option (5).

9. **(2) gracefully vigorous** (Literal Comprehension) This information is found in the last two sentences. Options (1) and (5) are contradicted in the text. There is no evidence for options (3) and (4).

10. **(2) there are not many powerful male dancers in ballet** (Inferential Comprehension)

That ballet needs more powerful male dancers is suggested in the first paragraph. There is no evidence for options (1), (3), or (4). The ballet is set in 1919, but was not written then.

11. **(3) A New Hero for the Ballet** (Application) O'Day is a hero, not only in this particular ballet, but as a new role model for ballet in general. Options (2), (4), and (5) are not supported. Option (1) refers to the plot of the dance being reviewed.

12. **(4) to suggest that ballet can be quite masculine** (Analysis) The author refers several times to the importance of the male image in the ballet. This review would have little impact on sales in separate cities (option 1). Options (2) and (3) are wrong because there is no support. O'Day seems to be an exception to the need for training (option 5).

13. **(3) has a happy ending** (Literal Comprehension) This information is stated in the words "happily-ever-after" (line 25). None of the other options is supported by the excerpt.

14. **(5) She is a successful ballet choreographer.** (Inferential Comprehension) Based on the fact that the author calls *Everlast* a "triumph" and the description of Tharp's experience in ballet, this is a logical conclusion. There is no support for options (1) and (4). Options (2) and (3) are contrary to the information given.

SIMULATED TEST A
(pages 62–72)

1. **(3) that Minta really had forgotten Brownie** (Inferential Comprehension) Earlier Minta had imagined herself saying she would never forget to feed Brownie, but she did forget. Although options (2) and (5) may be true, they are not important here. There is no evidence for options (1) or (4).

2. **(3) What Minta imagines her future to be is made clear to the reader.** (Analysis) The italics help to mark the difference between reality and Minta's imagination. Option (2) is wrong because the future described exists only in Minta's mind. Option (1) is about the past, not the future. There is no support for options (4) or (5).

3. **(4) a stabbing knife** (Literal Comprehension) Minta imagines being stabbed after the door is broken in. Options (1) and (2) do not fit thrusting steel. The description would be odd for option (3) and an awkward metaphor for option (5).

4. **(3) Mrs. Beal** (Literal Comprehension) It is Mrs. Beal at the door. Only in Minta's imagination are options (1) and (2) possible. Option (4) is wrong because the daughter is probably at home. There is no evidence for option (5).

5. **(3) She is no longer afraid to be alone in the house.** (Inferential Comprehension) Minta is brought back to warm reality and is no longer afraid; therefore, options (4) and (5) are wrong. There is no evidence for options (1) and (2).

6. **(5) a science fiction writer** (Inferential Comprehension) Smith is used as an example of science fiction writers who anticipate scientific achievements. There is no evidence that he was a scientist or was associated with actual space flight as suggested in the other options.

7. **(4) there is an intellectual relationship between science fiction and science fact** (Literal Comprehension) Asimov states that he does not believe options (1), (2), and (3). There is no support for option (5).

8. **(5) It would only reach the speed of light.** (Literal Comprehension) This information is stated in the first paragraph. Option (1) is too definite. Option (2) is not supported. Options (3) and (4) are true but are irrelevant to the question.

9. **(2) as a link between fact and imagination** (Analysis) Options (1) and (3) are wrong because he does not lead to a discussion of that question itself. Option (4) is wrong because Asimov simply states an opinion and then moves to a related topic. Option (5) is wrong because only one writer is cited as having trouble with the question.

10. **(4) deny something absolutely** (Literal Comprehension) This follows his denial and precedes a qualifying remark. Options (1), (2), (3), and (5) would not make sense in this context.

11. **(3) reads a lot of science fiction** (Inferential Comprehension) His references indicated he is well-read in the field. He does not believe science fiction writers are always accurate, but that doesn't mean he disapproves (option 1). Options (2) and (5) have no support. Option (4) is wrong because he uses himself as an example of the science fiction writer's mind.

12. **(5) the last line of the poem** (Analysis) The phrase is the beginning of an explanation of how the speaker can let go. Options (1) and (2) bear no relation to the phrase. The poet is trying to convey a much different idea than those in options (3) and (4).

13. **(4) loving regret** (Application) The speaker is anticipating the loss of her beloved, but all the while is continuing to love. Options (1), (2), (3), and (5) suggest emotions not expressed in the poem.

14. **(3) understanding in human relationships** (Application) All the other options deal with generalities. The poet appears to be more concerned with the nature of the individual.

15. **(4) She's thinking about how other lovers will see these things.** (Analysis) There is no evidence for options (1) or (5). Option (3) is wrong because of the complexity of the descriptions. Option (2) would lessen the impact of the poem.

16. **(2) brown** (Literal Comprehension) Copper pennies in dark honey are brown. There is no evidence for the other options.

17. **(5) preparing herself for being alone** (Inferential Comprehension) In recognizing that she cannot stop the person from leaving and in accepting the fact, she is preparing herself. There is no evidence for options (1), (2), or (4). The speaker is somewhat selfish in that she is letting go slowly, so option (3) is wrong.

18. **(3) in a kitchen** (Literal Comprehension) Options (1), (2), and (4) are not referred to in the directions. Option (5) is wrong because Mama crosses to the living room; we don't necessarily see her in it.

19. **(2) She would give Jessie only some of her attention.** (Application) Option (1) is the opposite of how Mama acts in this scene. There is no support for options (3), (4), or (5).

20. **(5) to make the audience wonder what Jessie is planning to do** (Analysis) The collection of items is odd enough to suggest that Jessie is planning something unusual. Options (1) and (2) have no support. Option (3) is incorrect because Jessie shows little concern about Saturday night. Option (4) is denied by Jessie.

21. **(3) by having them carry on what are almost two separate conversations** (Analysis) The two women do seem to be talking about different subjects, indicating that there is an emotional distance between them. Although they don't ignore each other, they also don't really pay attention. No support is given for options (1) or (2). Option (4) reveals something about Mama only. Option (5) is wrong because neither expresses any emotion.

22. **(4) redo her fingernail polish** (Literal Comprehension) Mama refers to her chipped fingernails; Jessie admits that doing Mama's nails is on the schedule. There is no support for the other options.

23. **(2) is fairly lazy** (Inferential Comprehension) Mama does not pick up the dessert wrapper or do her own nails. She also just took a nap. There is no support for options (1), (3), or (4). Option (5) is wrong because she nags Jessie.

24. **(3) plowing a field** (Literal Comprehension) Option (1) is wrong because the crop is not yet grown. Surgery (option 2) is a metaphor here for the impersonal plowing. Options (4) and (5) are opposite to the activity of the man in the excerpt.

25. **(3) Both the man and the bank see the land as a source of income.** (Inferential Comprehension) By pairing the man with the bank, the author suggests they have the same attitude. Neither the man nor the bank love the land, as suggested by options (1), (2), and (5). There is no evidence that the man even owns the land (option 4).

26. **(2) the tractor and the other farm machines** (Literal Comprehension) Although the seat is iron (option 1), so is the rest of the tractor. Options (3) and (4) are not mentioned in the text. The land is under iron, so option (5) is incorrect.

27. **(3) to suggest that a person must be emotionally involved in order for the land to thrive** (Analysis) Options (1) and (4) are wrong because the main idea is that land will die if treated impersonally. There is no evidence of why the man felt indifferent (option 2) or whether he was religious (option 5).

28. **(5) indifference** (Inferential Comprehension) The man is uninterested in anything about the land or what it produces; therefore, there is no support for options (1), (2), and (3). He admires only the machine (option 4).

29. **(2) the envy of the angels** (Analysis) The repetition of the angelic imagery is a clue to its importance. The speaker believes that even heaven was aware of the beauty of their love. Love is not made special by age (option 1), by death (option 3), by the cause of death (option 5), or by status (option 4).

30. **(4) continue to mourn his lost love** (Application) The speaker's moody reflection on Annabel Lee shows no sign of ending soon; therefore, option (1) is wrong. The speaker is estranged from her family (option 5), but option (2) is too extreme a reaction. The speaker actually resents the angel's interference, so option (3) is unlikely.

31. **(3) become the speaker's devoted wife** (Application) Annabel Lee's only thought was to love and be loved by the speaker. There is no evidence to suggest options (1) or (5). Options (2) and (4) suggest a type of selfishness that is not supported in the poem.

32. **(4) repeating "a kingdom by the sea"** (Analysis) Pay attention to repetition. This phrase occurs frequently and suggests mystery and romance because it reminds the reader of fairy tales without being specific. Although option (1) may contribute to the overall mood, it is secondary to the repetition motif. Options (2) and (3) do not create mood. Option (5) is wrong because we know the death was caused by a chill.

33. **(5) He still loves Annabel Lee.** (Inferential Comprehension) He speaks with passion about what happened many years ago. Apparently he is still obsessed with recalling the love they shared. There is no support for options (1), (2), (3), or (4).

34. **(3) an elaborate tomb** (Literal Comprehension) A noble person would have an elaborate final resting place. Options (1) and (4) are wrong because they suggest she is alive. Options (2) and (5) are wrong because of the phrase "shut up."

35. **(2) No major biographies of Robeson were published before Duberman's.** (Literal Comprehension) This is stated in the text. There is no evidence for options (1) or (5), and evidence is present to contradict options (3) and (4).

36. **(4) a supporter of the civil rights movement** (Application) Robeson, as a black man who feels

he has not been recognized as a human being, would have been involved in the civil rights movement that began to make headlines in the 1950's. The time difference would have had little effect on his personality (option 1) or his talent (option 3). There is no evidence for options (2) and (5).

37. **(2) Cesar Chávez** (Application) Cesar Chávez championed the cause for civil rights among Hispanic Americans. Robeson most likely would have admired a person who struggled against great odds and the status quo in order to gain equal rights and restore a sense of dignity to his people. Although options (3), (4), and (5) may have admirable qualities, they would probably have less appeal to Robeson. Hitler was a racial oppressor, a symbol of what Robeson hated (option 1).

38. **(1) that Robeson's story is a major example of a human problem** (Analysis) Robeson was wronged by two systems of belief, not one in particular, as suggested by options (2) and (5). Option (3) is not true. Option (4) is true but does not explain the phrase.

39. **(4) He was no longer allowed to leave the United States.** (Literal Comprehension) The reviewer states that Robeson was denied a passport. There is no evidence for the other options.

40. **(4) In the United States he felt trapped by racial prejudice.** (Inferential Comprehension) Robeson felt free, with his human dignity restored, when he visited the Soviet Union. There is no support for options (1), (2), or (5). Option (3) is wrong because the policy actively discouraged individual creativity.

41. **(1) an actual TV set and picture** (Analysis) the frame is the actual TV set with the portrait being the picture. Options (2), (3), and (5) are more abstract than is intended. Option (4) is not relevant to TV.

42. **(4) calm** (Literal Comprehension) Letterman is described as relaxed. None of the other options apply.

43. **(3) makes fun of silliness on TV** (Inferential Comprehension) Letterman's actions and attitudes reflect the opinion of many of today's viewers that very few current TV programs contain much of value. The other options may be true, but they do not explain the phrase.

44. **(5) ignore the basic reason for his popularity** (Inferential Comprehension) This idea is suggested in the last paragraph in which the reviewer contradicts options (1) and (4). Options (2) and (3) are wrong because the comments are favorable, not negative, and rather overstated.

45. **(5) as examples of efforts to define Letterman's personality** (Analysis) An example, rather than a lengthy explanation, often helps to clarify a statement. These examples indicate the manner in which people are writing about Letterman. The quotations do not function in the ways suggested in the other options.

SIMULATED TEST B
(pages 74–85)

1. **(2) Beauty and the Beast** (Application) Jerome is physically attractive and the woman is unattractive. There is no such contrast in options (1) or (3). The contrasts in (4) and (5) involve morality, not appearance.

2. **(3) The relationship will end unhappily.** (Application) The text suggests that falling in love with Jerome resulted in trouble, not happiness as in options (1) and (2). There is no evidence for options (4) or (5).

3. **(4) different than the woman's** (Inferential Comprehension) Jerome did not like the clothes she had purchased for him, so options (2) and (3) are wrong. There is no support for options (1) and (5).

4. **(3) she will leave him alone** (Inferential Comprehension) This is suggested by his promise to wear the suit he liked least. Options (1), (4), and (5) have no support. Option (2) is wrong because he hates what she has gotten already.

5. **(5) She has found what she is looking for.** (Literal Comprehension) She is searching Jerome's pockets but they are empty. All the other options are mentioned in the text.

6. **(1) Woodson is an expert with strong opinions.** (Analysis) Quotations from experts give support to a writer's point. Option (3) is not true. Option (4) is wrong because quotations aren't needed to provide examples. Options (2) and (5) have no support.

7. **(2) what is wrong with something** (Literal Comprehension) This meaning repeats the main idea of something being wrong. Options (1), (3), (4), and (5) do not make sense in this sentence.

8. **(3) to reinforce the analogy made in the first paragraph** (Analysis) Gray is not really a drummer. The phrase is a metaphor that refers back to Woodson's first example; therefore, options (1), (2), and (4) are wrong. She is an example of someone who succeeded, not someone who failed (option 5).

9. **(1) a study of unemployment among teenagers** (Application) Options (2), (3), (4), and (5) are examples of studying success. Only option (1) is an example of failure.

10. **(1) waste the public's money** (Inferential Comprehension) Social agencies are usually funded with public monies, so any wasted money would be the public's. There is no support for the other options.

11. **(2) gets money back because people at that project pay their rent regularly** (Literal Comprehension) This is stated in the text, so

option (1) is not true. Options (3) and (4) are unlikely given the circumstances. There is no evidence for option (5).

12. **(3) is abnormal** (Literal Comprehension) The onion is deformed, but neither frightens her (option 1) nor reminds her of a fairy tale (option 2). Option (4) wrongly gives it animation. There is no evidence for option (5).

13. **(3) a wife's frustration** (Analysis) The phrasing, such as "We cannot escape each other," (line 10) and the overall negative imagery underscore the speaker's frustration in relation to her marriage. There is no support for options (1), (2), (4), and (5).

14. **(5) breaking the bond between husband and wife** (Inferential Comprehension) This is a metaphor for the emotional bond between man and woman. Options (1), (2), and (4) are wrong because they are literal interpretations. There is no evidence to support option (3).

15. **(3) she feels that a connection holds them together** (Inferential Comprehension) The entire poem has led up to this suggestion. Option (1) is too literal an interpretation. There is no support for options (2), (4), or (5).

16. **(3) as a metaphor for the speaker's troubled marriage** (Analysis) The poem points to this marriage as an uncomfortable and unnatural union. The image of the mutant onion reinforces that idea. There is no evidence to support options (1) or (5). Neither option (2) nor option (4) applies.

17. **(5) suggests that men are unwilling to deal with emotional issues** (Analysis) The transparent onion skin is basic to the conclusions of the poem; so perhaps is the idea that a man might have been unable to perceive what is stated in the first stanza. There is no real support for options (1) and (3). Option (4) is not explained by the lines. Option (2) misses the point entirely.

18. **(3) agreeing to dance with her** (Literal Comprehension) This refers to Eugene's need to count as he dances. There is no evidence to support the other options.

19. **(4) in the army** (Inferential Comprehension) Eugene's learning to march and having to do push-ups both suggest this. Option (1) is wrong because he is clearly not much of a dancer. Option (2) is wrong because having the same first name as an author does not make him one. There is no evidence for options (3) or (5).

20. **(2) to show how Daisy and Eugene are supposed to move** (Literal Comprehension) Most of the directions refer to where the two are putting their hands and feet. Options (1) and (3) have no support. Option (4) is wrong because the directions are simple. Option (5) is wrong because the dialogue alone is not enough to suggest what is happening.

21. **(3) it is a way to start a conversation** (Inferential Comprehension) People usually tell their names, and that's as good a way as any to start a conversation. There is no support for options (1), (2), and (4). Option (5) is wrong because they haven't talked about anything else yet.

22. **(2) laugh at the couple** (Analysis) The dialogue is slightly silly and amusing. Option (1) is wrong because Daisy is doing fine. A vague coincidence of names is not enough to justify option (3). What is happening is not exciting enough to provoke options (4) or (5).

23. **(5) be friendly** (Application) The two are on fairly good terms here and probably will continue to be so. Nothing has occurred to embarrass either person (option 1), nor to justify an extreme emotional response as in options (2) and (3). There is no support for option (4).

24. **(4) story-teller** (Literal Comprehension) Raconteur refers to the previous sentence, in which men have made a living by telling stories. Part of the clue lies in understanding the transformation of the noun Orient into the adjective Oriental, which describes, not defines (option 2). Options (1) and (5) are wrong because they are not the ones who make a living this way. Option (3) is the thing told, not the teller.

25. **(2) as entertainment** (Inferential Comprehension) The word primarily in the question invalidates both options (1) and (3). There is no support for options (4) and (5).

26. **(5) by a scholarly researcher** (Analysis) This passage is in the third person, not the first (option 1). The historical evidence and analysis support the idea of research, not firsthand experience (option 4). Options (2) and (3) have no support.

27. **(3) when putting a child to sleep** (Application) It is still more common to put a child to sleep by telling stories than by telling jokes. Options (1), (2), (4), and (5) are all likely situations in which the telling of jokes would be appropriate.

28. **(5) A Story for One and All** (Application) Folktales appear to please almost everyone. Option (1) represents only one example, not the main idea. Options (2) and (3) have no support. Option (4) is wrong because it applies only in a few instances.

29. **(1) told in different languages and about different cultures** (Inferential Comprehension) Folktales have been told all over the world and so would be told in ways appropriate to each society. There is no evidence here for option (2). Options (3), (4), and (5) are wrong because the content is not mentioned.

30. **(3) to attract the men's attention** (Inferential Comprehension) Coughing is a way to attract attention, and that is what these women want. There is no support for options (1), (2), or (5).

Option (4) is incorrect because the men are apparently not looking at them.

31. **(4) to demonstrate how casual they are** (Inferential Comprehension) Although the whistling might annoy the women, the more important interpretation is that the men appear to be relaxed and unconcerned with whatever is bothering the women. There is no support for the other options.

32. **(5) to make the audience laugh** (Analysis) This is a silly remark (option 1), and it bears no relation to repentance (option 2). Eating muffins has little to do with sensitivity (option 3) or the time of day (option 4). That anyone could see eating muffins as a sign of repentance is funny.

33. **(3) Gwendolen will be the first to speak.** (Application) These women are neither as dignified nor as aloof as they would like to pretend. As they very much want the men's company, Gwendolen will probably "break the ice" that the men aren't even aware of. Options (1), (4), and (5) are not in accord with the women's characters. Option (2) is wrong because it disregards the men's casual attitude.

34. **(1) English upper class** (Inferential Comprehension) The group speaks in formal language which one would suspect of that social level. There is no support for option (2). The one song does not suggest option (3), nor do the muffins suggest option (4). There is no evidence for option (5).

35. **(4) outdoors** (Literal Comprehension) The sketch was done in the backyard, eliminating Options (1), (3), and (5). Crane also states he doesn't use photographs (Option 5). There is no support for Option (2).

36. **(4) "Backyards are like portraits."** (Analysis) Crane feels that landscape reflects a human presence and doesn't need the figure. Options (1), (2), and (5) have nothing to do with figures. Option (3) refers to technique, not content.

37. **(3) immediately providing the reader with descriptive images** (Analysis) Option (3) steers the reader back to the text where multiple examples are given. Options (1), (2), (4), and (5) are only factors that are best summed up by the examples.

38. **(1) linking her conclusion to her introduction** (Inferential Comprehension) These words refer back to her phrase "seethe with life of the moment" and so give unity to the paragraph. She enjoys the vigor of the paintings, so Option (2) is incorrect. Option (3) refers to what Crane says. Option (4) is incorrect because she is expressing her own opinion. Option (5) has no support.

39. **(2) alive** (Literal Comprehension) The reviewer is referring to the liveliness and sense of humanity. There is no support for the other options.

40. **(3) People occasionally enjoy escaping from reality.** (Inferential Comprehension) This is suggested by Copperfield's earlier comment about people's desire to escape into fantasy. Option (1) is not true. Option (2) is not addressed. There is no evidence to support option (4) or option (5).

41. **(4) stay more alert on stage** (Literal Comprehension) Copperfield states this is his remedy for not paying enough attention, so option (1) is wrong. Dangerous acts do not appear to have any relationship to options (2), (3), or (5).

42. **(2) donating time to a local children's home** (Application) The magician's involvement with people who have disabilities suggests a charitable nature. Options (1), (4), and (5) have no support. Option (3) is wrong because he is already quite motivated.

43. **(3) to set up a difference between illusion and reality** (Analysis) The author first mentions illusions but wants to lead into the actual nature of the performances. Options (1), (2), and (4) are wrong because they imply a belief that magic really works. The statement is not an example of amazing magic (option 5).

44. **(2) anything he does on TV he can do onstage** (Literal Comprehension) Copperfield states this in the sixth paragraph in order to discourage the ideas in options (1) and (3). There is no evidence for options (4) or (5).

45. **(3) to demonstrate his understanding of the psychology of magic** (Analysis) Copperfield very clearly states that he understands the nature of both the magic tricks and the social value of illusion. The reviewer gives no suggestion of options (1) or (4). Option (2) is wrong because, first, she doesn't know his secrets and, second, his comments are about something else entirely. Option (5) is incorrect because Copperfield is quite straightforward; only his magic mystifies.

Suggestions for Additional Reading

The following lists contain recommended readings. These sources contain excellent examples of writing of the type you will encounter in the GED Interpreting Literature and the Arts Test.

Popular Literature

General
The New Yorker
Atlantic Monthly

Fiction
Best American Short Stories
Erma Bombeck, *If Life is a Bowl of Cherries, Why Do I Always Get the Pits?*
Stephen King, *Insomnia*
The Signet Classic Book of Contemporary American Short Stories, ed. Burton Raffel
Amy Tan, *The Joy Luck Club*
John Kennedy Toole, *A Confederacy of Dunces*
Robert James Waller, *The Bridges of Madison County*

Nonfiction
Maya Angelou, *I Know Why the Caged Bird Sings*
Best American Essays
Dee Brown, *Bury My Heart at Wounded Knee*
Shelby Foote, *The Civil War: A Narrative*
John Hersey, *Hiroshima*
Deborah Tannen, *You Just Don't Understand*
Studs Turkel, *Race*
Malcom X with Alex Haley, *The Autobiography of Malcom X*

Poetry
Maya Angelou, *Complete Poems*
Best American Poems
Gwendolyn Brooks, *Blacks*
Flowering After Frost: An Anthology of Contemporary New England Poetry, ed. Michael Mahon
Langston Hughes, *Selected Poems of Langston Hughes*
Sylvia Plath, *The Colossus and Other Poems*
Elinor Wylie, *Collected Poems*

Drama
Best American Plays
Alan Bennett, *The Madness of King George*
Robert Bolt, *A Man for All Seasons*
Sam Shepard, *Seven Plays*
Tom Stoppard, *Rosencrantz and Guildenstern Are Dead*

Classical Literature

Fiction
Stephen Crane, *The Red Badge of Courage*
Charles Dickens, *A Christmas Carol*
F. Scott Fitzgerald, *The Great Gatsby*
Ernest Hemingway, *The Short Stories of Ernest Hemingway*, *The Old Man and the Sea*
Jack London, *The Best Short Stories of Jack London*
Richard Wright, *Native Son*

Nonfiction
Ruth Benedict, *Patterns of Culture*
Joseph Campbell, *The Hero with a Thousand Faces*
Anne Frank, *The Diary of a Young Girl*
Carl Sandburg, *Abraham Lincoln: The Prairie Years*

Poetry
British and American Poets: Chaucer to the Present, ed. Charles Hirschfield
The Poem: An Anthology, ed. Stanley Greenfield and A. Kinsley Weatherhead
T.S. Eliot, *The Waste Land and Other Poems*
Walter de la Mare, *Collected Poems, 1901–1918*

Drama
American Drama, ed. Alan S. Downer
Anton Chekhov, *Uncle Vanya*
Henrik Ibsen, *Four Great Plays*
Luigi Pirandello, *Naked Masks*
Tennessee Williams, *A Streetcar Named Desire*, *Cat on a Hot Tin Roof*

Commentary on the Arts

General
Chicago Tribune
Dallas Morning News
Entertainment Weekly
Houston Chronicle
Los Angeles Times
Newsweek
The New Yorker
New York Times
Time
USA Today
Village Voice
the entertainment section of your favorite newspaper

Literature
The New York Review of Books
New York Times Book Review

TV and Film
TV Guide
Video Review

Visual Arts
American Artist
Art in America

Performing Arts
Down Beat
Opera News
Rolling Stone
Vibe

Acknowledgments

Grateful acknowledgment is made to the following authors, agents, and publishers for permission to reprint copyrighted materials.

Alfred A. Knopf, Inc.; from *Word Play What Happens When People Talk* by Peter Farb. Copyright 1973 by Peter Farb. **(p. 15)**

Arcade Publishing, Silko, Leslie Marmon. "How To Write a Poem About the Sky," copyright © 1981 by Leslie Marmon Silko. Reprinted from STORYTELLER by Leslie Marmon Silko, published by Seaver Books, New York, NY. **(p. 25)**

Art in America and Peter Clothier; from "Herb Elsky at Jan Baum" by Peter Clothier in *Art in America* magazine, Oct. 1986, p. 176. **(p. 58)**

Curtis Brown, Ltd. for "Splitting Wood At Six Above" by Maxine Kumin. Reprinted by permission of Curtis Brown, Ltd. Copyright © 1982 by Maxine Kumin. First published by the Viking Press. **(p. 18)**

Ceramics Monthly; from "Wedgwood Then and Now" in *Ceramics Monthly* magazine, May 1988, p. 71 & 79. **(p. 56)**

Kay Collyer & Boose; from *Rich and Famous* by John Guare. Copyright © 1977 St. Jude Productions, Inc. **(p. 28)**

The Chicago Tribune; from "Human Sacrifices to the god of War" by David E. Jones in *The Chicago Tribune*, April 4, 1989, Sec. 2, p. 3 © Copyrighted, Chicago Tribune Company, all rights reserved. **(p. 50)** From "Stupid Emcee Tricks" by Rick Kogan in *The Chicago Tribune*, April 30, 1989, p. 13. © Copyrighted, Chicago Tribune Company, all rights reserved. **(p. 72)**

The David Company; "The Bean Eaters" from *The Blacks*, by Gwendolyn Brooks. Used by permission of the author. **(p. 22)**

Delacorte Press; from *Player Piano* by Kurt Vonnegut, Jr. Copyright © 1952 by Kurt Vonnegut Jr. Reprinted by permission of Delacorte Press/Seymour Lawrence, a division of Bantam, Doubleday, Dell Publishing Group, Inc. **(p. 10)**

Doubleday, a division of Bantam, Doubleday, Dell Publishing Group, Inc.; from "Sonny's Blues" in *Going to Meet the Man* by James Baldwin. Copyright © 1957 by James Baldwin. **(p. 11)** From *Mary, Mary* by Jean Kerr. Copyright © 1963 by Jean Kerr. **(p. 31)** "Even As I Hold You" from *Goodnight Willie Lee, I'll See You In the Morning* by Alice Walker. Copyright © 1978 by Alice Walker. Reprinted by permission of Bantam, Doubleday, Dell Publishing Group, Inc. **(p. 65)**

Dramatists Play Service for excerpt from JOINED AT THE HEAD by Catherine Butterfield, © Copyright, 1993, by Catherine Butterfield. CAUTION: The reprinting of JOINED AT THE HEAD included in this volume is reprinted by the permission of the author and Dramatists Play Service, Inc. The stock and amateur performance rights in this play are controlled exclusively by Dramatists Play Service, Inc., 440 Park Avenue South, New York, NY 10016. No stock or amateur production of the play may be given without obtaining in advance, the written permission of the Dramatists Play Service, Inc., and paying the requisite fee. Inquiries regarding all other rights should be addressed to Gilbert Parker, William Morris Agency, Inc., 1325 Avenue of the Americas, New York, NY 10019. **(p. 27)**

E. P. Dutton; from *The Chamber Plays* by August Strindberg. Copyright © 1962 by Evert Sprinchorn and Seabury Quinn, Jr. Reprinted by permission of the publisher, E. P. Dutton, a division of Penguin Books USA, Inc. **(p. 46)**

Farrar, Straus and Giroux, Inc.; from "The Jewbird" in *Idiots First* by Bernard Malamud. Copyright © 1963 by Bernard Malamud. Reprinted by permission of Farrar, Straus and Giroux, Inc. **(p. 7)**

Harcourt Brace Jovanovich, Inc.; from "Her Sweet Jerome" in *In Love and Trouble*, copyright © 1970 by Alice Walker. **(p. 75)** From "The Death of the Moth" in *The Death of the Moth and Other Stories* by Virginia Woolf, copyright 1942 by Harcourt Brace Jovanovich, Inc. and renewed 1970 by Marjorie T. Parsons. **(p. 36)** From "A Child's Day" in *Cress Delahanty*, copyright 1953 by Jessamyn West. **(p. 63)** From "Introductory" in *Aspects of the Novel* by E. M. Forster, copyright 1927 by Harcourt Brace Jovanovich, Inc. and renewed 1955 by E. M. Forster. All reprinted by permission of Harcourt Brace Jovanovich. **(p. 38)**

Harper & Row, Publishers, Inc.; "That Moment" from *New Selected Poems* by Ted Hughes. Copyright © 1982 by Ted Hughes. **(p. 21)**

HarperCollins Publishers for excerpt from PIGS IN HEAVEN by Barbara Kingsolver. Reprinted by permission of HarperCollins Publishers. **(p. 5)**

Henry Holt and Company; "Bereft" by Robert Frost copyright 1927 by Holt, Rinehart and Winston, renewed 1956 by Robert Frost. Reprinted from *The Poetry of Robert Frost*, edited by Edward Connery Lathem. **(p. 43)** "Is My Team Plowing" by A. E. Housman copyright 1939, 1940, © 1965 by Holt, Rinehart and Winston. Copyright © 1967, 1968 by Robert E. Symons. Reprinted from *The Collected Poems of A. E. Housman*. By permission of Henry Holt and Company, Inc. **(p. 41)**

Hill & Wang, a division of Farrar, Straus and Giroux, Inc.; from *'Night Mother* by Marsha Norman. Copyright © 1983 by Marsha Norman. Reprinted by permission of Farrar, Straus and Giroux, Inc. **(p. 66)**

Holt, Rinehart & Winston; from *The Folktale* by Stith Thompson, copyright 1946 by Holt, Rinehart and Winston, reprinted by permission of the publisher. **(p. 81)**

The Indianapolis Star; "Magician Finds His Shows Hard Work" by Anja Freyer in *The Indianapolis Star*, April 12, 1989, p. B9. **(p. 84)**

Carol Kleiman; "My Home Is Not Broken, It Works." Copyright 1984 by Carol Kleiman. Reprinted by permission of the author. **(p. 14)**

Ellen Levine Literary Agency, Inc. for excerpt from FRAGMENTS OF THE ARK by Louise Meriwether. Copyright © 1994 by Louise Meriwether. Reprinted by permission of the author and Ellen Levine Literary Agency, Inc. **(p. 8)**

Little, Brown and Company for excerpt from DREAM MAKERS, DREAM BREAKERS by Carl T. Rowan. Copyright © 1993 by CTR Productions, Inc. By permission of Little, Brown and Company. **(p. 12)**

Liveright Publishing Corporation; "maggie and milly and molly and may" is reprinted from *Complete Poems, 1913-1962* by E. E. Cummings, by permission of Liveright Publishing Corporation. Copyright © 1923, 1925, 1931, 1935, 1938, 1939, 1940, 1944, 1945, 1946, 1947, 1948, 1949, 1950, 1951, 1952, 1953, 1954, 1955, 1956, 1957, 1958, 1959, 1960, 1961, 1962 by the Trustees for E. E. Cummings Trust. Copyright © 1961, 1963, 1968 by Marion Morehouse Cummings. **(p. 44)** "Those Winter

Sundays" is reprinted from *Angle of Ascent, New and Selected Poems* by Robert Hayden, by permission of Liveright Publishing Corporation. Copyright © 1975, 1972, 1970, 1966 by Robert Hayden. **(p. 20)**

Louisiana State University Press; "A Poem for Emily" from *Imperfect Love* by Miller Williams. Copyright © 1983, 1984, 1985 by Miller Williams. Originally appeared in *Poetry*. **(p. 19)**

MCA Publishing Rights, a Division of MCA Inc.; from *Going My Way* by Frank Butler and Frank Cavett. Copyright © by Paramount Pictures. Courtesy of MCA Publishing Rights, a Division of MCA Inc. **(p. 30)**

Hilary Masters for excerpt from "Lucinda Matlock" from SPOON RIVER ANTHOLOGY, copyright 1944 by Edgar Lee Masters. Reprinted by permission of Hilary Masters. **(p. 40)**

Methuen, a division of Octopus Publishing Group; from *Educating Rita* by Willie Russell. Copyright 1981 by Willie Russell. **(p. 29)**

The Muncie Star, from "Historian Sheds Light on Ruebens and Art of Portraiture" by Nancy Millard in *The Muncie Star*, December 18, 1989, p. B11. Copyright *The Muncie Star*. **(p. 57)**

Mundus Artium and Reiner Schulte; "Conjoined" by Judith Minty from *Mundus Artium*, Vol. VII, No. 2. **(p. 78)**

News America Publishing for "The adventures of 'Andre'—a deal with a splashy appeal" by Ray Stackhouse from TV Guide dated 8/19-25/95 **(p. 53)**, and "Murphy Brown" by Jeff Jarvis from TV Guide dated 8/12/95. 1995 Copyright, News America Publications, Inc. (TV Guide Magazine). **(p. 54)**

Newsweek, Inc.; from "Taking the High Road" by David Ansen, in *Newsweek* magazine, Dec. 19, 1988, p. 57. © 1988 Newsweek, Inc. **(p. 55)** From "Fun and Games in the Windy City" by John McCormick in *Newsweek* magazine, Feb. 27, 1989, p. 72 © 1989 Newsweek, Inc. **(p. 51)** from "Transforming the Landscape" by Cathleen McGuigan in *Newsweek* Magazine, Dec. 26, 1988, p. 82, © 1988 Newsweek, Inc. **(p. 83)** From "An American Tragedy" by Jim Miller in *Newsweek* magazine, Feb. 13, 1989, p. 78, © 1989 Newsweek, Inc. **(p. 70)** From "Where Are All the Men?" by Laura Shapiro in *Newsweek* magazine, April 10, 1989, p. 63, © 1989 Newsweek, Inc. **(p. 61)**

The New York Times Company; from "Truth Isn't Stranger Than Fiction, Just Slower" by Isaac Asimov, in *The New York Times*, June 5, 1983. Copyright © 1983 by the New York Times Company. **(p. 69)** From "Poor Russell's Almanac" by Russell Baker in *The New York Times*, Oct. 16, 1969. Copyright © 1969 by the New York Times Company. **(p. 16)** From James M. Cornelius of *Legends, Lies and Cherished Myths of American History* in *The New York Times*, Dec. 18, 1988. Copyright © 1988 by the New York Times Company. **(p. 49)**

Ohio University Press/Swallow Press; 8 lines from the poem "Lisa" by Constance Carrier, copyright The Swallow Press, 1955. Reprinted with permission of the Swallow Press. **(p. 24)**

Peggy Pfau for excerpt from THE MAGNIFICENT AMBERSONS by Booth Tarkington. By permission of National City Bank, Indiana, Agent for Tarkington Literary Properties. **(p. 33)**

Penguin Books USA, Inc. for excerpt from "My Left Foot", copyright © 1989 by Pauline Kael. Originally appeared in the New Yorker; from MOVIE LOVE: COMPLETE REVIEWS by Pauline Kael. Used by permission of Dutton Signet, a division of Penguin Books USA, Inc. **(p. 52)**

Random House, Inc. for "Life Doesn't Frighten Me At All" from AND STILL I RISE by Maya Angelou. Copyright © 1978 by Maya Angelou. Reprinted by permission of Random House, Inc. **(p. 26)**

Random House, Inc.; from "Was" reprinted from *Go Down Moses* by William Faulkner. Copyright 1942 by William Faulkner. **(p. 34)** From *The Canadians* by Andrew Malcolm. Copyright © 1985 by Andrew Malcolm. **(p. 17)** From *Biloxi Blues* by Neil Simon. Copyright © 1986 by Neil Simon. This play or any portion therof cannot be performed, recited, recorded, or broadcast in any media without a license from the author. **(p. 79)**

St. Martin's Press for excerpt from SLOW BURN by Eleanor Taylor Bland. Copyright © 1993 by Eleanor Taylor Bland. Reprinted by permission of the publisher. **(p. 8)**

The Society of Authors on behalf of the Bernard Shaw Estate; from *Major Barbara* by Bernard Shaw, Copyright © 1941 by Bernard Shaw. **(p. 45)**

Carolyn N. Swayze for excerpt from "Mankiewitz Won't Be Bowling Tuesday's Anymore" from SHOELESS JOE JACKSON COMES TO IOWA by W. P. Kinsella. Copyright © 1980 by W. P. Kinsella. First published by Oberon Press. Reprinted by permission of Carolyn N. Swayze, Barrister & Solicitor, WRAPS, White Rock, BC, Canada. **(p. 4)**

Swenson, May; "Painting the Gate" by May Swenson. ©1976 by May Swenson. **(p. 23)**

Time, Inc. for excerpt from "Grief and Rebirth/Interview With Isabel Allende," © 1995 Time, Inc. Reprinted by permission. **(p. 48)**

USA TODAY for "Country world heeds her clear siren song" copyright USA TODAY. Reprinted with permission. **(p. 59)**

Viking Penguin, a division of Penguin Books USA, Inc.; from *The Grapes of Wrath* by John Steinbeck. Copyright 1939, renewed © 1967 by John Steinbeck. **(p. 67)** From *Sometimes a Great Notion* by Ken Kesey. Copyright © 1963, 1964 by Ken Kesey. **(p. 7)**

The Village Voice; from "Meredith Monk Ancient Lullabies" by Kyle Gann in *The Village Voice*, Dec. 27, 1988, p. 91. **(p. 60)**

Kal Wagenheim for excerpt from *Clemente*. Originally published in 1973 by Praeger Publishers. Copyright © 1984 by Waterfront Press, Maplewood, NJ. Used by permission of the author.

Washington Post Writers group; from "We Can Learn Little By Studying Failure" by William Raspberry. Copyright 1985, Washington Post Writers Group. **(p. 76)**

Watkins/Loomis Agency, Inc.; from "Are Women Human?" in *Unpopular Opinions* by Dorothy Sayers, Copyright 1974, by Dorothy L. Sayers. **(p. 37)**

Wylie, Aitken & Stone; from *Train Whistle Guitar* by Albert Murray. Copyright © 1974 by Albert Murray. **(p. 6)**

Answer Sheet

GED Literature and the Arts Test

Name: _____ Class: _____ Date: _____

○ Simulated Test A   ○ Simulated Test B

1 ①②③④⑤	9 ①②③④⑤	17 ①②③④⑤	25 ①②③④⑤	33 ①②③④⑤	41 ①②③④⑤
2 ①②③④⑤	10 ①②③④⑤	18 ①②③④⑤	26 ①②③④⑤	34 ①②③④⑤	42 ①②③④⑤
3 ①②③④⑤	11 ①②③④⑤	19 ①②③④⑤	27 ①②③④⑤	35 ①②③④⑤	43 ①②③④⑤
4 ①②③④⑤	12 ①②③④⑤	20 ①②③④⑤	28 ①②③④⑤	36 ①②③④⑤	44 ①②③④⑤
5 ①②③④⑤	13 ①②③④⑤	21 ①②③④⑤	29 ①②③④⑤	37 ①②③④⑤	45 ①②③④⑤
6 ①②③④⑤	14 ①②③④⑤	22 ①②③④⑤	30 ①②③④⑤	38 ①②③④⑤	
7 ①②③④⑤	15 ①②③④⑤	23 ①②③④⑤	31 ①②③④⑤	39 ①②③④⑤	
8 ①②③④⑤	16 ①②③④⑤	24 ①②③④⑤	32 ①②③④⑤	40 ①②③④⑤	